Leona Sumrall Murphy
USING·THE
POWER
of
PRAYER

Printed 1987

Unless otherwise indicated, all Scripture quotations are taken from the *King James Version* of the Bible.

USING THE POWER OF PRAYER
ISBN 0-937580-06-6
Copyright © 1987 by
Leona Sumrall Murphy
Published by LESEA Publishing Company
P.O. Box 12
South Bend, Indiana 46624

Printed in the United States of America.
All rights reserved under International
Copyright Law. Contents and/or cover may
not be reproduced in whole or in part in any
form without the express written consent of
the Publisher

DEDICATED TO MOTHER SUMRALL

Her prayers go from adoring whispers to torrential outpourings of verbal groans and strong tears. Then there were times her prayers would be calm and comforting, eloquent, routine and heart-warming.

CONTENTS

GOD'S SECRETS 9
PRAY BY ASKING 19
PRAY BY SEEKING 34
PRAY BY KNOCKING 49
PRAYING IN THE SPIRIT 63
PRAYER CREATES FAITH 78
PRAYER AND FASTING 94
PRAYER BRINGS REVIVAL 111
GROANS, AGONY & TRAVAIL 129

1

GOD'S SECRETS

The Apostle Paul stated in II Corinthians 12:3-4, *And I knew such a man, (whether in the body, or out of the body, I cannot tell: God knoweth;) How that he was caught up into paradise, and heard unspeakable words, which it is not lawful for a man to utter.*

In reading this scripture it leads us to believe that silence concerning some things brings greater glory to God than proclamation.

The tendency of so many today is to immediately publish abroad anything that God would give in gifts, ministries or revelations; and there is almost an equal inclination to tell publicly of any ministry to the Lord in tithing, fasting, etc.

Generally speaking a person that spends

many hours in prayer never reveals that which God has shown about another, but prays through to victory and then puts it in the back of their minds. Having things revealed to pray about is not the same as the gift of knowledge. The problem is that some intercessors cannot keep spiritual revelation in confidence. They relate what God has shown them. By the time the revelation has passed through several people the picture cannot be recognized. This is where self-denial really comes in. If an intercessor "REVEALS" what has been shown him, he should be very certain that it is the Holy Spirit guiding him and not his own spirit (Proverbs 16:32).

If a man or woman breaks confidence, then God will have to shut off revealing things to him until he learns to keep God's secrets. There are some who have done this and learned quickly and corrected themselves. Others are so eager to have these revelations that they will go to any end to have them. In their desire to have something to tell, they will listen to any voice. They make an opening for Satan to come to them as an angel of light and the devil's revelations will cause trouble because they are false (II Corinthians 11:14).

1. If God reveals something in the church that is wrong, then that person should pray.

2. An intercessor should never usurp the authority of the pastor. If the Holy Spirit desires to use his intercession to help the pastor in dealing with situations in the church, he should obey.
3. The intercessor will have been able to pull down strongholds of Satan and make for smoother sailing for the church.

In reading the twelfth chapter of Paul's second epistle to the Corinthians, you may have wondered at the very unusual statement of verses three and four: *"And I knew such a man, (whether in the body, or out of the body, I cannot tell: God knoweth;) how that he was caught up into paradise, and heard UNSPEAKABLE WORDS, which it is not lawful for a man to utter."*

In Paul's brief statement, he undoubtedly refers to a most tremendous spiritual experience in his own life. So real was this visit to paradise, the apostle could not tell whether he was in the spirit or in physical presence. We would have every reason to expect Paul to devote much time and space to a detailed account of this thrilling visit to paradise, but the unusual truth is that Paul refuses to comment. Without apology or excuse, the apostle simply states that the words he heard were "UNSPEAKABLE" and were "not lawful for a man to utter."

We read in II Timothy 3:16 that "All scripture is given by inspiration of God, and is profitable...for instruction in righteousness." Perhaps God would bring to us a lesson of instruction from Paul's experience and testimony.

It is true that most testimonies commence or climax with the statement, "We tell this for the glory of God," but the Scripture leads us to believe that some things are not to be told.

We read in Luke 24:34, *"The Lord is risen indeed, and hath appeared to Simon."* PETER HAD DENIED HIS LORD at the house of Caiaphas the night of His betrayal, and then with bitter tears he had followed afar off. The darkness and gloom of defeat that fell like a cloak over Peter was only lifted when Jesus arose and appeared to him personally. This personal appearance that Christ made alone to Peter must have been one of the most outstanding experiences influencing Peter's future life and ministry, but Peter personally remains silent concerning this precious experience that he enjoyed with the Master alone.

Could anything be greater than the

experience which befell Mary, the Mother of Jesus? We read in Luke 1:26-28, *The angel Gabriel was sent from God unto a city of Galilee, named Nazareth, to a virgin espoused to a man whose name was Joseph, of the house of David; and the virgin's name was Mary. And the angel came in unto her, and said, Hail, thou that are highly favoured, the Lord is with thee: blessed art thou among women.* Mary did not immediately make a canvas of Nazareth to inform everyone that Gabriel had appeared to her. Instead, of those days when the hand of God was mightily upon His handmaiden, we read in Luke 2:19, *But Mary kept all these things, and pondered them in her heart.*

When Elisha came to the crucial moment of his experience when Elijah was to be taken from him, we read in II Kings 2:11, *And it came to pass, as they still went on, and talked, that behold, there appeared a chariot of fire. . .* From the standpoint of human interest, could anything be more desirable than to know the final conversation between Elijah and Elisha on that memorable day when the chariot of fire carried Elijah to glory, and the mantle of power was granted to Elisha? As much as man might desire to know the last words of Elijah to Elisha, the Scripture simply states, "They talked together," nor does Elisha volunteer any further comment on the message of this last hour with Elijah which marked the beginning of his ministry of power.

We read in Judges 14:5-6, *Then went Samson down, and his father and his mother, to Timnath, and came to the vineyards of Timnath; and, behold, a young lion roared against him. And the spirit of the LORD came mightily upon him, and he rent him as he would have rent a kid, and he had nothing in his hand: but he told not his father or his mother what he had done.* The loss of this anointing and strength came about when Samson began telling what God had done for him. We read in Judges 16:17, *He told her all his heart,. . .* and the moment that Samson told everything to Delilah the enemy began to lay a snare which eventually brought his downfall.

Anointed eloquence comes from the pen of Paul in Hebrews 11:32-33, *And what shall I more say? for the time would fail me to tell of Gedeon, and of Barak, and of Samson, and of Jephthae, of David also, and Samuel, and of the prophets: Who through faith subdued kingdoms, wrought righteousness, obtained promises, stopped the mouths of lions. . .*

God is anxious today to grant faith and

spiritual power to His servants, that they might do exploits for their God.

The great need today is for men who will treasure dearly and use wisely what God may give. We find no illustrations in the Word where men of great power spent time announcing what God had given into their hands, but we do hear from Paul's lips the emphatic statement of Romans 14:22, *Hast thou faith? have it to thyself before God. . .*

We have the words of Jesus in John 5:44, *How can ye believe, which receive honour one of another, and seek not the honour that cometh from God only?*

Fasting is definitely scriptural, but there is certainly no scripture in the Word of God which licenses us to announce to others that we are fasting, or have been fasting, or expect to fast. Jesus plainly states in Matthew 6:17-18, *But thou, when thou fastest, anoint thine head, and wash thy face; that thou appear not unto men to fast, but unto thy Father which is in secret. . .*

Tithing is most certainly scriptural, but the Bible warns us concerning drawing attention to ourselves in our giving, for we read in Matthew 6:1, *Take heed that ye do not your alms before men, to be seen of them: otherwise ye have no reward of your Father which is in heaven.*

It is scriptural to expect an assurance of the answer to our prayers when we pray, but it is wise to carefully consider the nature of the assurance that God gives before you pass it on to others. When Nehemiah received the assurance from God regarding the rebuilding of Jerusalem, he could have enthusiastically announced to all of his friends the fact that God had revealed to him the plan for rebuilding Jerusalem. But we read in Nehemiah 2:12, *. . . neither told I any man what my God had put in my heart to do at Jerusalem. . .*

Men who are truly close to God will soon learn that there are some things that God will entrust as secrets, which are not to be told to others. God spoke of Daniel as a man "dearly beloved" and, as in the lives of others, so Daniel too, is heard to state in Daniel 7:28, *. . . but I kept the matter in my heart.*

The Scripture certainly encourages us to "covet earnestly the best gifts." If ever there was a man anointed of God and blessed with spiritual gifts in operation in his ministry, it was Paul. Paul remained a great blessing through the years of his ministry because he continued to recognize a very important divine principle, stated in I Corinthians 1:29, *That no flesh should glory in his presence.* Paul's instructions to others may be found in such scriptures as I Corinthians 4:7, *For who maketh thee to differ from another? and what hast thou that thou didst not receive? now if thou didst receive it, why dost thou glory, as if thou hadst not received it?* Undoubtedly there were those in Paul's day who received special gifts and ministries of the Lord and immediately commenced to proudly announce what God had given. Paul's correction to such is rather severe, in this same fourth chapter, verses 19-20, *But I will come to you shortly, if the Lord will, and will know, not the speech of them which are puffed up, but the power. For the kingdom of God is not in word, but in power.*

John the baptist sent his disciples to Jesus with the question that we find in Matthew 11:3, . . . *Art thou He that should come, or do we look for another?* In the reply that Jesus brought to this question, there is no reference to Himself. He simply turns the attention of the questioning men to the results of His ministry. As Christ gives the example, so likewise He also gives the instruction for us to follow. We read in Matthew 5:16, *Let your light so shine before men, that they may see your good works, and glorify your Father which is in heaven.* If a man is walking with God, he should not have to tell the world what he possesses; the fruit of his life and the results of his ministry should cause men to behold and glorify, not the individual, but the Father which is in heaven.

God's Word tells us in Ecclesiastes 3:7 that there is. . . *a time to keep silence, and a time to speak.* . . A good question for every true servant of Christ to ask before he speaks is, "Do my words cause men to see self, or Christ?" Let us remember that the great desire of those around us is still formed in the words of John 12:21, . . . *Sir, we would see Jesus.*

2

PRAY BY ASKING

*And in that day ye shall ask me nothing.
Verily, verily, I say unto you,
Whatsoever ye shall ask the Father
in my name, he will give it you.*
(John 16:23)

Asking is the basic prayer to build a foundation with God to further advance into other levels of prayer.

While having family devotion we were taught the gifts of Jehovah are available for the asking and that God is willing to give His children the answer.

My first experience of asking and receiving was when I was five years old.

Mother was in the mercantile business and had gone to town on business, taking me along. As we passed a furniture store I pointed to the store window. With excitement in my voice I said, "Mother, look!" Stopping, she looked in the direction I was pointing. There was a little rocking chair just my size. I said, "Please mother, buy that chair for me." She said, "You have a nice rocking chair at home." I said, "But mother, I like the chair in the store window." She tried to reason with me, but I did not want to listen.

When we arrived home, I was brokenhearted. The family wanted to know why I was crying. Mother told how we had passed a furniture store and I saw a rocking chair. She said, "She has a good chair and I am not going to buy another one." I was not able to influence mother but I won the family's sympathy.

Mother always prayed in her bedroom, so I went to her bedroom. I prayed, "Dear Jesus, give me that little rocking chair. Mother refuses to buy it for me, but I know, Jesus, you will give it to me." I reminded the Lord I had served him all my life, which was the long period of five years.

My uncle, who was a traveling salesman, was passing through. Since he was near our town, he decided to stop for two or three hours. When he came in he asked, "Where is Leona?" Mother said "She is praying!" He asked, "What is her problem?" Mother told him about our experience with the rocking chair. He opened the door, came over to the bed, put his arms around my shoulders and said, "Why all the tears?" I looked up, then I really turned on the tears. After hearing my story, he said, "You are going to have that chair and you are going to get it today, if an old devil like me has to buy it!"

We went to town and returned home with the chair. God desires to give good things to those who ask Him. Matthew 7:11, *If ye then, being evil, know how to give good gifts unto your children, how much more shall your Father which is in heaven give good things to them that ask him?*

In prayer, we must learn to ask! Although it is true that God knows everything, we cannot develop the attitude that there is no need to ask anything from God because He already knows what we need. Some have come to the conclusion that we should not ask because of the verse found in Matthew 6:8, *Be not ye therefore like unto them: for your Father knoweth what things ye have need of, before ye ask him.*

However, the context of the verse just quoted is most important in understanding the verse. Jesus had first said in Matthew 6:7, *But when ye pray, use not vain repetitions, as the heathen do: for they think that they shall be heard for their much speaking.* Therefore, repeating the same prayers ritualistically was what Jesus was referring to. He did not intend for us not to ask, as we shall see later; but, on the contrary, He intended us to ask our Father with prayers that proceed from our heart.

Petitioning God is basic to prayer! God is our Father; and as a Father, He enjoys giving to His children. A child has rights in a family. God's Son, Jesus Christ, commanded us in strong language in John 16:23-24, . . . *Verily, verily, I say unto you, Whatsoever ye shall ask the Father in my name, he will give it you. Hitherto have ye asked nothing in my name: ask, and ye shall receive, that your joy may be full.*

In verse 27, Christ shows why this works: *For the Father himself loveth you, because ye have loved me, and have believed that I came out from God.* The Father loves us because we believe in His Son. Therefore, we are partakers of the inheritance of the only begotten Son of God.

Christ came to this world to bring redemption

and restoration to fallen man. When Christ hung on the cross, the Father was bringing about the conditions through which mankind could be restored unto complete fellowship with his God. Paul stated in II Corinthians 5:19, *To wit, that God was in Christ, reconciling the world unto himself, not imputing their trespasses unto them; and hath committed unto us the word of reconciliation.* Based upon the reconciling work of the Father, we all have the potential for salvation. Yet, salvation must be preached throughout the ends of the earth, giving all men the opportunity to accept or reject the gospel—the Good News that the price has been paid and direct access to God is available to all men. Mankind has to ask and receive this great blessing of salvation. A man must ask Christ to forgive his sins through repentance. He must ask Christ to enter his heart. Although the gift of salvation is there for everyone, it can only be appropriated by asking.

Not only is our regeneration the product of asking for what was purchased for us; but, also, the Holy Spirit's fullness is available simply by asking. Luke 11:13, . . .*how much more shall your heavenly Father give the Holy Spirit to them that ask him?* Therefore, the gift of salvation, the fullness of the Holy Spirit, as well as all other gifts are available through petitioning prayer.

James states that God will not refuse anyone who asks Him for wisdom, but will give it freely—as long as it is asked in faith (James 1:5). The gifts of the Holy Spirit are available for the asking. Healing, deliverance, prosperity and blessing are all to be asked for. We also have a right to ask for revival, Zechariah 10:1, *Ask ye of the LORD rain in the time of the latter rain; so the LORD shall make bright clouds, and give them showers of rain. . .* The blessing of God is ours for the asking. We can have God's blessings, typified in Zechariah as rain because God has commanded us to ask for them.

It becomes obvious that God is willing to give to His children; however, we must participate actively in the answer to our needs by asking.

How does asking work? How can we get our prayers of petition answered?

There are four conditions that must be met to get assurance that our petitions as Christians will be answered affirmatively:

1. We must ASK IN FAITH! Simply asking God for things will not assure you of a positive response. Matthew 21:22, *And all things,*

whatsoever ye shall ask in prayer, believing, ye shall receive.
2. We must ABIDE IN A RELATIONSHIP with Christ! John 15:7, *If ye abide in me, and my words abide in you, ye shall ask what ye will, and it shall be done unto you.* When we abide in prayer, we develop spiritually so that His desires are ours; therefore, this spiritual blank check can be entrusted to us.
3. We must be MOTIVATED PROPERLY! James 4:3, *You ask, and do not receive, because you ask amiss, that you may spend it on your pleasures* (NKJV). It is God's desire to give us all good things. We know that, yet, so many requests are generated by sheer selfishness. God desires that what we ask should be to the end that He may be glorified.
4. We must ASK IN ACCORDANCE WITH THE WILL OF GOD! Does this mean that we should wonder whether God wants us healed before we pray for healing? No! This is why knowledge of Scripture is so important. The Bible tells us what the will of God is, so, when we ask for something that God has promised us, then we know with certainty that we are praying in God's will: I John 5:14-15, *Now this is the confidence*

that we have in him, that if we ask anything according to his will, he hears us. And if we know that he hears us, whatever we ask, we know that we have the petitions that we have asked of him (NKJV).

How does God answer our petitions? God responds to our requests within the framework of His personality. That is, He does not just give us exactly what we need; on the contrary, He gives to us in abundance. Philippians 4:19, *And my God shall supply all your need according to His riches in glory in Christ Jesus* (NKJV). God's resources are unlimited resources. In this way, He supplies all of our needs. Therefore, God is not lacking in any good thing. He has a storehouse full; we can learn how to open the storehouse by knowing how to petition.

I learned these principles in the early days of my ministry. I studied the Scriptures and discovered that God is a good God. During the most difficult economic depression, I began my ministry. I learned how to fast—not because I was spiritual, but because I had nothing to eat! Yet, through prayer and Bible study, I discovered that God is not just the God of America and Europe; God is the God of anyone who will learn to trust Him.

I have told this story many times. Yet it perfectly illustrates the way to get your petitions answered from our Father.

Lester and I were both teenagers, while conducting a revival in Shawnee, Oklahoma. The pastor's wife invited me to go with her to town. As we walked down the sidewalk we passed a shoe store. My attention was drawn to a pair of shoes in the show window. Upon our return to the parsonage I went directly to my brother Lester's room. He had always been liberal toward me. I told him about the shoes—looking up from his Bible, he asked, "What do they cost?" They were expensive! He shook his head in the negative, saying his car payment was due, and there would be no money left for shoes.

The first night of the revival, the pastor asked for a 24 hour prayer chain. I agreed to pray the noon hour. It was time for me to pray so I went to the church. The first prayer I prayed, I asked God to give me the shoes I had seen in the store window that morning. I prayed until I felt the assurance. It was as though I could almost feel the shoes on my feet. Then I prayed for the revival. A little after 1:00 PM I returned to the parsonage. The pastor's wife said I had received a telephone call and a member of the church would be by later to take me some place. I asked if she could describe the lady. She began by saying that she is a good lady but a little strange. She sat alone and did not talk to very many people. No one seemed to dislike her and no one seemed to like her.

Soon I heard a strange noise. I looked out and there stood an old Model "T" Ford. I asked, "Who is that?" The pastor's wife said, "That is the lady that telephoned." We were soon on our way. It sounded as though every bolt in the car was loose and the fenders might fall off at any moment. We were driving to parts unknown as far as I knew. After driving a few blocks, she said, "I was praying this morning. Just before noon the Lord told me to buy you something." I will have to admit this frightened me. I asked, "Did the Lord tell you what to buy?" She said, "No." Very meekly I asked, with fear and trembling. "Did He tell you the amount you were to spend?" She said "Yes!" She quoted the exact price of the shoes. If my brother thought the shoes were too expensive, what would this little lady think? I knew I had better do some praying or she would be offended. My heart almost stopped as she parked in front of the store where the shoes were displayed. I could hardly get out fast enough. Looking toward me she suggested we walk down to the store where she shopped. I was a little shy but I assured her what I wanted was in THIS store. When I pointed to the shoes, the salesman said, "Those are sample shoes and we only have the one pair. The one in the window." He asked my size. I NEEDED BIG ONES AND HE SAID THESE WERE SMALL ONES. I knew if God had worked this far, the shoes had to fit. With much persuasion he took a long pole and fished the shoes out of the window. All the time he was saying, "They are not your size." The man said with a puzzled look on his face, "We never put a size larger than a 5 in the window, and you take several sizes larger." He said, "I do not understand it." I understood. To the salesman's surprise when he went to put the shoes on they were a perfect fit. I do not know when God stretched the shoes to my size, but I knew it was an answer to my prayer.

When God miraculously provided for the shoes, I was made to rejoice. In this way, God taught me to be specific in my petitions. This is how to pray in faith. Do not pray in generalities! Know what you need! Tell God in detail exactly what you are asking for! Then, begin to confess that you have received it! You may not want to do it in public, but begin to thank God and confess the answer! Remember that what we ask in faith, God will provide. It was important for God to teach me this early in my ministry.

Usually, only preachers in large churches talk about God's abundance in providing for their needs. But, I can testify that God can do the same for any man or woman who will petition God according to His Holy Word.

So often our economic conditions dictate our faith level. This is why it is so important for us to ask God to increase our visions and dreams, which are the language of the Holy Spirit. By having a greater vision we can see the greater provision of God.

I have heard it said, "that great men must come from great countries, live in great times, and perform great tasks." This is normally true. However, Jesus Christ, the Son of God, came from a small and weak country, Israel. At the time of our Lord's coming, Israel was under the oppression of the Roman Empire. Although He performed the greatest of tasks, He certainly did not live in a great time for Israel. Yet He is the focal point of human history.

No matter who you are, you can make a difference! Your life can change your town, nation and the world—if you know the secret of petitioning prayer.

Solomon said in Proverbs 18:16, *A man's gift maketh room for him, and bringeth him before great men.* God desires to give you much more than you can dream or imagine. Ask God for the gift that will cause you to have the greatest effect on your situation! Do not be satisfied with the status quo! I came from a poor home; and from poor natural circumstances. I have never had to force my way into good churches. The gracious gift that God has given me has brought me into many nations of the world. If God can do this for me, He can do this for you too! As you are reading this book know that your life can make an imprint upon those around you. Have faith that no matter in what location you find yourself, God may desire to use you in great revival fires that will sweep the world.

Ask, and you will receive!

God told Moses in Deuteronomy 4:29, *But if from thence thou shalt seek the LORD thy God, thou shalt find him, if thou seek him with all thy heart and with all thy soul.*

Man has been created to desire communion with God. There is a void that cannot be filled by anything but genuine communion with

God. No matter what man acquires, it cannot replace the fellowship that fulfills the very essence of man's being—giving purpose to like and nourishing his soul.

God created Adam and gave him the breath of life. He was a physical being before he was a spiritual being. Adam's spiritual dimension gave him the capacity for communion and fellowship with God in the midst of the garden, in the cool of the evening. Man lost his ability through sin, but God still desired to fellowship with man, so He took the initiative with Abraham. Abraham became the father of the faithful who would have the opportunity to fellowship with God.

Then God revealed His physical presence on earth in the Tabernacle of Moses. However, with few exceptions, only the High Priest could enter into the third part of the Tabernacle of Moses which was called the Holy of Holies.

When David was finally recognized as king of Israel, his first act was to bring the Ark of the Covenant, the symbol of God's presence, back to the center of Israel's worship. However, rather than place it in Moses' tent, God requested that he erect one in Zion, the place where David had his personal home, Psalm 132:13, *For the LORD hath chosen Zion; he hath desired it for his habitation.* In Zion, God would have direct access and communion with Israel.

However, the worship of Israel again became the object of ritual. God again took the initiative to restore fellowship with man when He came in the person of Jesus Christ.

In the Church Age, we have been given the Holy Spirit to lead us into fellowship and communion with the Father and Son. Jesus said in John 16:14-15, *He shall glorify me: for he shall receive of mine, and shall show it unto you. All things that the Father hath are mine: therefore said I, that he shall take of mine, and shall show it unto you.* Jesus further amplifies in John 14:21, . . .*he that loveth me shall be loved of my Father, and I will love him, and will manifest myself to him.* Then in the twenty-third verse He said, *If a man love me, he will keep my words: and my Father will love him, and we will come unto him, and make our abode with him.*

3

PRAY BY SEEKING

*Seek ye the LORD while he may be found,
call ye upon him while he is near.*
Isaiah 55:6

Having invited us to seek Him, He tells us He is not sought in vain. Prayer is important in getting what we need from God, but there is more to prayer than asking. Jesus said, *Seek and ye shall find!* Therefore, the next level of prayer beyond "asking" is "seeking." This in no way discounts asking. The seeking does not discount the praying, but the praying is always included in the seeking.

The reason for seeking God is that we owe it to Him. We were not created for ourselves, but for His glory. God as Creator is fully entitled to derive great happiness from His creatures. His greatest happiness comes from our happiness in Him. Since there is joy in the presence of the angels whenever one sinner repents, it is evident that God's happiness can be increased by men seeking Him.

The eagerness of God for man's search for Him is demonstrated by all the efforts God has made to bring about reconciliation between man and Himself. This is seen from the very first when God provided an atonement for man in the Garden of Eden all the way down to the Cross where God exhibited to all the world His infinite love for man by the sacrifice of His Son. It is further seen by His many invitations to man to seek Him.

God responds to those who seek Him. However, this seeking must not be a mere halfhearted effort. Assurance for success is given only to those who are wholehearted. Jeremiah 29:13, *Ye shall seek me, and find me, when ye shall search for me with all your heart.* We seek Him wholeheartedly when we do not permit anything or anyone to interfere.

This seeking must be kept up with diligence. Hebrews 11:6, *...and that he is a rewarder of them that diligently seek him.* A DILIGENT

SEEKER IS ONE WHO SEEKS GOD WITH PERSISTENCE. Luke 11 tells of two friends and how one denied the other his request for three loaves of bread because he came at an inopportune time. It also tells of how the one friend persisted in his request until the other gave it to him. This does not mean that God will deny our request, but it does mean that we are to persist even though God does not seem to respond. He will respond if we do not give up.

Luke 11:9-10, *Ask, and it shall be given you; seek, and ye shall find; knock, and it shall be opened unto you. For every one that asketh receiveth; and he that seeketh findeth; and to him that knocketh it shall be opened.* We are exhorted to ASK, SEEK, AND KNOCK with the assurance of a response from Him.

These three statements are not synonymous in meaning. They are steps. They constitute three phases or degrees in our search for God.

The first has to do with PETITION, the stating of our specific request. This means that we know what we are after. Vague generalities are ineffectual. If we need bread, we must ask for bread; and if we need the Holy Spirit, we must ask for the Holy Spirit. Luke 11:10, *Every one that asketh receiveth.*

But asking is not wishing. There must be a

genuine sense of a well-defined need, and that need should be specifically mentioned. If we need healing of the gall bladder, we do not ask for a "touch in body." That is too general. We must know what we want, must want what we know we need, and must state the need to God specifically and expectantly.

Seek, and ye shall find. This has to do with believing expectancy.

Several years ago we made a pilgrimage to the Holy Land with a religious group. This was the first time for our guide to lead a tour to Israel. Before leaving the United States he failed to make reservations for us to leave Egypt.

We landed in Egypt after midnight. A tour bus took us to a native hotel. When we saw our rooms the windows had wooden shutters that opened out on the streets. I had just taken off my dress when an Egyptian man walked into my room. He could not speak English and I could not speak Egyptian. He closed my suitcase and signaled me to follow. I followed him down the hall without shoes or a dress on. When my husband returned and found I was gone he went looking for me. As he passed down the hall heads began peeping out of their doors. One man said he could not find his aunt. The Egyptian decided to move her too.

When Jim found the aunt she was very angry. She said, "Look at this tub! Would you bathe in it? I think they washed the mop out and left the sand in the bottom of the tub."

Going to breakfast was another experience. The men waiters were barefooted. Their aprons and tea towel, which were once white, were now gray. The man that poured our coffee had a cold and he used the cloth for his nose. Before pouring the coffee he used the same towel to dry the inside of my cup.

The following day as we were touring the city our guide left the bus to establish our time of departure. It was then that he was notified that there had been no reservations made for us to leave Egypt. The owner of the tour company had a representative in Egypt that we contacted. When our guide from the United States got back on the bus he was pale and nervous. He called my husband aside and told him the bad news. We would have to return to the same hotel for the night. My husband said, "No, we are not." Turning to the bus driver he said, "Take us to the Hilton Hotel." With a lot of bargaining we managed to keep our group in this first class hotel overnight. We were told our only other choice was to fly into Lebanon.

The next morning we flew into Beirut. When

we arrived we saw many buildings demolished from gun fire. Men were running in the streets with guns. We were taken to a hotel to spend the day. That night we were to catch a British plane out of the country. All the stores around the hotel were closed. We were their only guests. The workers they called to prepare our food saw some of the people outside sitting around the pool. We were warned that a sniper could be watching from an adjoining building. Near the end of the day we were told our bus would be coming to take us to the airport in two hours. The group began to get nervous. A few of us found a place to pray.

When others of the tour group saw we were praying they joined us. The longer we prayed the more we knew our lives were in danger. Several of us entered into a spirit of intercession and were praying in our prayer language. When the bus arrived we were urged to load as fast as possible. Once we were out into the countryside where there was no traffic, several car loads of men stopped the bus. As we looked out the window we could see that large metal spikes blocked the road. One of the men opened the bus door on the driver's side, pulled the driver out onto the ground and hit him in the stomach with the butt of his gun. The driver collapsed on the ground. We knew we were going to be taken as hostages and would perhaps lose our lives. At this time, I looked out and saw an army truck drive up. I learned later that the army had heard of the plot to capture the tour bus and take the people as hostages. They surrounded the bus, took the keys from the terrorist and lifted up the driver and put him back inside. The soldier handed him the keys and said, "Don't stop until you reach the airport." They pulled the metal spikes out of the road and we passed through. When we arrived at the airport one hour later we were told the group should stay close together going from the bus to the terminal. We all learned the power of seeking God for protection. We knew the Holy Spirit had sent His angels to protect us.

Notice how willing God is to have us come to Him in our need. This is very closely connected with another indispensable necessity: FAITH. Hebrews 11:6, *Without faith it is impossible to please him; for he that cometh to God must believe that he is, and that he is a rewarder of them that diligently seek him.*

There is a direct relationship between our faith (or lack of it) and our conscience. I John 3:21, *Beloved, if our heart condemn us not, then have we confidence toward God.* Acts 24:16 tells us that a strong faith demands *a conscience void of offense toward God, and toward men.*

I often tell people if you go to a store to buy bread, do you state your request and walk out at once? Wouldn't that be absurd? Yet this is precisely what many people do with God. They state their requests and away they go. It is true we cannot stay on our knees all the time. But, it is also true that having made our petition to God, we can go about our normal duties with an attitude of expectancy and anticipation. This expectant attitude is the difference between real seeking and mere wishing.

The third statement, "Knock, and it shall be opened unto you," is the kind of praying that brings results. Note that the seeker is here pictured as being at the threshold. He does not have far to go nor long to wait. He has started with asking, continued with seeking, and ends with presistence which will not take no for an answer; his responsibility is merely to be there as the earnest, believing petitioner. The door is opened by someone within, not by the petitioner from outside.

We know that there is a reward for seeking. In seeking God we must not get the idea that God will reward us for our effort in the sense that He will repay us for the time and sacrifice, or coming to Him, or going to church. This is man's duty, his "reasonable service." The seeker is rewarded by having God do for him that which would not otherwise be done. God is so pleased by man's search for Him that He responds by placing Himself within reach of searching man. God Himself has assumed this responsibility.

Jeremiah 29:14, *I will be found of you, saith the LORD.*

Lamentations 3:40, *Let us search and try our ways, and turn again to the LORD.*

One of our difficulties in receiving things from God is that we come to Him with our own program and timetable. What makes things still more difficult, both for us and for God, is the mistaken use of scripture to prove our point.

For instance, we might think that if we fast and pray for four days as Cornelius did, we too shall be favored by the appearance of an angel. Or that because Daniel mourned 21 days and ate no pleasant food until he received an answer, we shall accomplish spectacular results by means of a semi-fast for 21 days. Merely copying such a pattern does not work.

If God uses passages of scripture to guide us in particular cases, that is another matter.

But, to arbitrarily select such as our own pattern is utterly false. In the first place, the underlying condition and motivation is missing. There is the matter of DIVINE PURPOSE to be considered. God leads us as individuals in a way that will compliment our personality. He is concerned about our circumstances. And He has a purpose concerning us. John 21:22, *If I will that he tarry till I come, what is that to thee? follow thou me.* This is a personal walk by means of personal guidance by a personal God.

Naaman the leper had a preconceived plan of how God was going to meet him. When God wanted to heal him in an unorthodox manner, he *was wroth, and went away, and said, Behold, I thought, He (Elisha) will surely come out to me, and stand, and call on the name of the LORD his God, and strike his hand over the place, and recover the leper* (II Kings 5:11) Naaman would have remained a leper had he not accepted God's own method, however humiliating it was and however strange it must have seemed to him.

It is delightful to learn the ways of the Lord, but the greatest delight is to learn that His ways are past finding out (Romans 11:33). When we think we have found the way in which God works, there is the mistaken belief that God is going to continue in the same way. Then we discover to our dismay that this is not God's way. It is our rut, and we might be buried in it unless we are ready to follow Him along other paths and thereby discover that His mercies are new every morning.

The subjective reason for seeking God is that we need Him. Man has been so created that without Him he is incomplete and therefore entirely devoid of true happiness. The rightly motivated seeker will not simply want to feel better; he will want to be better. He will not merely seek blessings; he will seek the Blesser.

Even where both motives and objectives are faulty, God attempts to meet us along the lines of our highest good. For this reason, He will first put His finger on things that are out of harmony with the holiness of God. In this we should find one of our greatest encouragements when we seek God. It means that God is working on the case, and the sooner we espond in obedience, the sooner we shall attain our objective. As we continue to seek and respond, God will continue with His response, and we shall find to our great delight the materialization of the glorious promise; Jeremiah 29:13-14, *Ye shall seek me. . .and I will be found of you, saith the LORD.*

The Apostle Paul lived his life in communion and prayer with Christ. To the church at Philippi he testifies in Philippians 3:7-8, *But what things were gain to me, those I counted loss for Christ. Yea doubtless, and I count all things but loss for the excellency of the knowledge of Christ Jesus my Lord: for whom I have suffered the loss of all things, and do count them but dung, that I may win Christ.* How could Paul win Christ? Remember that salvation is the gift of God, by faith, through grace. What Paul is referring to in Philippians 3 is more than receiving Christ in salvation; it is coming into a deep fellowship and communion. This type of prayer is not given freely. It must be sought after, thereby requiring effort. What did Paul receive from this type of prayer? He gives the answer in the tenth verse: *That I may know him, and the power of his resurrection, and the fellowship of his sufferings, being made comformable unto his death. And again, I press toward the mark for the prize of the high calling of God in Christ Jesus.* (v. 14).

In the fifteenth verse, Paul challenges all of us; *Let us therefore, as many as be perfect* (mature) *be thus minded. . .* Paul reveals in this verse that the sign of spiritual maturity is to desire to attain the spiritual level whereby we enter an intimate fellowship and communion with Christ. God is love. Love requires satisfaction through fellowship and communion. Therefore, God's very nature requires that we have the privilege and the ability to give Him communion.

In Colossians, Paul pictures the Church as a treasure field. In the field is hidden great treasure. Yet, the treasure is not material; it is spiritual wisdom and knowledge.

When young Christians pray, they normally approach the throne of God in time of need. Therefore, they go to God wanting something. God wants us to ask. Yet, many view Christ simply as a supermarket to which they can bring their shopping list and have all the items on it filled. However, all of the great mysteries, the treasures of understanding, the source of total and complete joy, the essence of love, are waiting as hidden treasure in Christ. Those who are wise will sell all and buy the field so they may gain the treasure.

Moses said in Deuteronomy 29:29, *The secret things belong unto the LORD our God: but those things which are revealed belong unto us and to our children for ever. . .* There is that which everyone can see in Scripture, but God wants to bring us into such close communion with

Himself that He may share His most intimate treasures of wisdom and understanding. Treasure would not be treasure if it were easily accessible. Therefore, God's spiritual treasure must be sought in prayer.

I learned many years ago that it takes effort to get the treasures that God desires to give me: Proverbs 8:17-19, *I love them that love me; and those that seek me early shall find me. Riches and honour are with me; yea, durable riches and righteousness. My fruit is better than gold, yea, than fine gold; and my revenue than choice silver.*

The lazy Christian is not willing to seek. He never enters into the fullness of the blessing which God desires him to have. It takes discipline and effort to live life at the doorpost of the Lord.

Why do people come to church? They come to be fed the meat of the Word of God. Where do I receive my messages? I get them from my Lord in prayer and intimate communion and fellowship. This is imperative for all wise Christians. Proverbs 8:33-35, *Hear instruction, and be wise, and refuse it not. Blessed is the man that heareth me, watching daily at my gates, waiting at the posts of my doors. For whoso findeth me findeth life, and shall obtain favour of the LORD.*

If your Christian life is not exciting, you have not learned to seek the Lord. If your study of the Word of God does not bring fresh insight into spiritual reality, then you have not entered this place of prayer. Seek and ye shall find!

4

PRAY BY KNOCKING

*For every one that asketh receiveth;
and he that seeketh findeth;
and to him that knocketh it shall be opened.*
Matthew 7:8

A door is used as an entrance to a house or a building. We knock because we have an urgent desire to enter.

While growing up, on the wall of our home hung a copy of the beautiful painting by Hoffman of Jesus standing on the outside of the door, knocking. Jesus taught us the importance of knocking. The three prayer worlds tell the story of your life. By understanding the three types of prayers, we can pray more effectively.

When a person is born spiritually, he is in the

first prayer world, "Give me, Lord" asking . . .Petition.

As he develops into the second prayer world, He seeks after the better things. . .God's will!

The third prayer world is knocking. Then he becomes a full adult Christian.

Knocking illustrates determination. Jesus gives us a perfect outline with two parables of prayer. The first was about a man who needed three loaves of bread at midnight. Jesus said in Luke 11:5-10, *Which of you shall have a friend, and shall go unto him at midnight, and say unto him, Friend, lend me three loaves. For a friend of mine in his journey is come to me, and I have nothing to set before him? And he from within shall answer and say, Trouble me not: the door is now shut, and my children are with me in bed; I cannot rise and give thee. I say unto you, Though he will not rise and give him, because he is his friend, yet because of his importunity he will rise and give him as many as he needeth. And I say unto you, Ask, and it shall be given you; seek, and ye shall find; knock, and it shall be opened unto you. For every one that asketh receiveth; and he that seeketh findeth; and to him that knocketh it shall be opened.*

But I'll tell you this—though he won't do it

Pray By Knocking

as a friend, if you keep knocking long enough he will get up and give you everything you want—just because of your persistence. And so it is with prayer—keep on knocking and you will keep on getting; keep on looking and you will keep on finding; knock and the door will be opened. Everyone who asks, receives; all who seek, find; and the door is opened to everyone who knocks.

Determination is the key to successful prayer. Prayer is not merely words; it is warfare. To knock is to storm the throne of grace and persevere and mercy will come down. Jesus said, . . .*men ought always to pray, and not to faint.* To faint means to give up, to quit. The lesson is plain: TO FAINT IS TO FAIL!

Jesus told another parable that corresponds with the one of the man asking for bread at midnight. This parable is of the widow who sought justice from an unjust judge. Jesus said in Luke 18:2-8, *There was in a city a judge, which feared not God, neither regarded man: And there was a widow in that city; and she came unto him, saying, Avenge me of mine adversary. And he would not for a while: but afterward he said within himself, Though I fear not God, nor regard man; Yet because this widow troubleth me, I will avenge her, lest by her continual coming she weary me. And the Lord said, Hear what the unjust judge saith. And shall not God avenge his own elect, which cry day and night unto him, though he bear long with them? I tell you that he will avenge them speedily. Nevertheless when the Son of man cometh, shall he find faith on the earth?*

Jesus reminds us again of the importance of perseverance. Many people ask this question: "If God is loving, why does He make things difficult?" If you want to get results, you must stay with it. Your commitment to get an answer will not only move God, it will change you from a spiritual weakling into a strong soldier for Jesus Christ!

Prayer is not overcoming God's reluctance; it is laying hold of His highest willingness. God is more than willing to move on your behalf if you will only take hold of His promises.

King David fasted and prayed that his son by Bathsheba would live. The Bible says in II Samuel 12:15-24, *And Nathan departed unto his house. And the LORD struck the child that Uriah's wife bare unto David, and it was very sick. David therefore besought God for the child; and David fasted, and went in and lay all night upon the earth. And the elders of his house arose, and went to him, to raise him up from the* earth: but he would not, neither did he eat bread with them.

And it came to pass on the seventh day, that the child died. And the servants of David feared to tell him that the child was dead: for they said, Behold, while the child was yet alive, we spake unto him, and he would not hearken unto our voice: how will he then vex himself, if we tell him that the child is dead? But when David saw that his servants whispered, David perceived that the child was dead: therefore David said unto his servants, Is the child dead? And they said, He is dead. Then David arose from the earth, and washed, and anointed himself, and changed his apparel, and came into the house of the LORD, and worshipped: then he came to his own house; and when he required, they set bread before him, and he did eat. Then said his servants unto him, What thing is this that thou hast done? thou didst fast and weep for the child, while it was alive; but when the child was dead, thou didst rise and eat bread. And he said, While the child was yet alive, I fasted and wept: for I said, Who can tell whether God will be gracious to me, that the child may live? But now he is dead, wherefore should I fast? can I bring him back again? I shall go to him, but he shall not return to me. And David comforted

Bathsheba his wife, and went in unto her, and lay with her: and she bare a son, and he called his name Solomon: and the LORD loved him.

David fasted and prayed for seven days, while the baby lay on the brink of death, before he reconciled himself to God's decision. He held onto God with determination. This is just one instance in David's life that reveals why God loved him so very much. David was known as a man after God's own heart.

The stress David suffered from the death of his son gave comfort to my parents.

It was past the midnight hour when Mother finally went to bed. She had fasted for days at a time and prayed hundreds of prayers for my father's salvation, all seemingly in vain. There seemed no way to reach him with the convicting power of the Holy Spirit.

By now Mother was awaiting their eighth child. When it came time for the child to be born, it was the easiest birth she had ever given. In fact, the power of the Holy Spirit came upon her and she began to speak in tongues the very instant the baby was born.

Mother and Papa called their new son Archie, and he was soon the pride and joy of the whole family. A big robust baby, he seemed perfectly normal in every way. Suddenly, however, he began losing weight so my parents consulted the family doctor. He thought the baby looked undernourished, but when they tried to force him to eat, he would become nauseated.

This was quite a shock to everyone since Archie had always seemed strong as he crawled and walked around in his play pen. Preachers and other Christians visiting our home would say, "This child, no doubt, is anointed with the Holy Ghost."

From his birth, Archie was loved by all the neighbors as he was a very friendly child. Each day, when it was time for Papa to come home from work, Archie would patiently watch the street corner. He would peep through the lattice work of his play pen and as soon as Papa would turn the corner, he would scream and call out to him. My father could hardly wait to get to the porch and hold Archie in his arms. Then he would hug and kiss him and call him "Daddy's boy."

All of the family became alarmed as they saw the little fellow grow weaker and thinner, yet never failing to have a beautiful smile on his face. The doctor came time after time only to say he could not understand why the child would not eat. He said that Archie's bones were beginning to become brittle from lack of calcium.

One day, after examining the baby, the doctor said to my father, "Mr. Sumrall, I have done all I can do for the baby. He is getting worse and I do not expect him to live."

After the doctor had assured him that Archie was not going to live, Papa tried to pray, but it seemed as though God was a thousand miles away.

The night the baby died, my father's heart was breaking. He went into the older boys' bedroom and fell across the bed in tears. As he lay there, his huge body racked with sobs, his little son suddenly appeared before him. He was so real that my father started to reach out to grab hold of him. All he could reach was thin air. In anguish my father cried out, "I want him, God. I want him!" But a voice from heaven announced, "You can go where he is, but you cannot bring him back to earth."

At those words, Papa jumped up from the bed and raced into the living room just in time to see the doctor pulling the sheet up over the face of his little boy. Archie had just returned to the Giver of Life.

It was a large funeral. People all over the vast audience were sobbing. Friends were standing out on the porch and in the yard. Mother sat by the side of the little casket and felt as though she was floating three feet in the air. She was not weeping, but rejoicing. God had lifted her above death and the grief that goes with it.

After the funeral was over and the procession was entering the cemetery, suddenly God spoke to Mother. He told her that Archie's brief visit here would prove to be the turning point of his father from sin to salvation. And it was!

Many times my father would tell the story of his beloved Archie, and with tears in his eyes he would always end by saying, "God told me that I could not bring Archie back, but He promised me that I could go where he is. I am living for God, and one day I will see my little son again."

A door is used as an entrance to a house or building. A door is used as the entrance into any spiritual experience, or the entrance to opportunity. Therefore, Jesus said, "I am the door." Christ is the means by which man can reach the Father. Paul used the word as an entrance to opportunity. What door do we enter in prayers of intercession?

Paul said in II Corinthians 2:12-13, *Furthermore, when I came to Troas to preach Christ's gospel, and a door was opened unto me of the Lord, I had no rest in my spirit...*

John, when writing to the church at Philadelphia, shares this revelation from Christ in Revelation 3:8, *I know thy works: behold, I have set before thee an open door, and no man can shut it...*

Not only is a door a place of opportunity to preach the gospel of Jesus Christ to a community; it is also an opportunity for an individual, as the Lord confirms in Revelation 3:20, *Behold, I stand at the door, and knock: if any man hear my voice, and open the door, I will come in to him, and will sup with him, and he with me.*

As the doors are opened, we are able to receive. We read in Acts 14:27, *And when they were come, and had gathered the church together, they rehearsed all that God had done with them, and how he had opened the door of faith unto the Gentiles.*

Going through a door of opportunity means we will face spiritual opposition from the principalities and powers that keep nations from hearing and responding to the gospel: I Corinthians 16:9, *For a great door and effectual is opened unto me, and there are many adversaries.*

Only the Lord Jesus Christ can open a door that has been shut to the gospel: II Corinthians 2:12, *Furthermore, when I came to Troas to preach Christ's gospel, and a door was opened unto me of the Lord...*

To get the doors of faith and opportunity opened, we have to know that Christ must open the door. However, God has made us members of His body. That means that the Head has chosen to function through His body on earth. So it takes prayers of intercession to stand against the spiritual forces keeping the doors shut. Once the prayers break through, Christ can open the door and an entire city, nation, or race can be saved. Paul confirms this: Colossians 4:3-4, *Withal praying also for us, that God would open unto us a door of utterance, to speak the mystery of Christ, for which I am also in bonds: That I may make it manifest, as I ought to speak.*

Not only does Christ desire to open doors of opportunity to His people, so they may preach the gospel but, doors of revelation and understanding must also be opened. Jesus continually repeats the phrase: "He that has ears, let him hear!" This statement made to the churches in Revelation chapters 2 and 3 indicates that we often do not understand what we are hearing. The door of understanding must be opened for our minds to comprehend what God desires to reveal to us: Revelation 4:1-2, *After this I looked, and, behold, a door was opened in heaven: and the first voice which I heard was as it were of a trumpet talking with me; which said, Come up hither, and I will show thee things which must be hereafter. And immediately I was in the spirit...*

In Acts we see how God can open a door of opporunity and keep the door open so we may preach the gospel without spiritual hindrance. Paul had been accused and had been brought to Rome, a city which was at that time the center of sin. Paul prayed and asked others to intercede for him. Finally, the door to Rome was opened: Acts 28:30-31, *And Paul dwelt two whole years in his own hired house, and received all that came in unto him, Preaching the kingdom of God, and teaching those things which concern the Lord Jesus Christ, with all confidence, no man forbidding him.* So, the Book of Acts ends. It is important that the Holy Spirit closes the Book of Acts with an open door.

Of course, most of us know that Acts ends without the proper grammatical ending. We can ascertain from this flaw (Luke, being a doctor, had an excellent command of Greek) that the Book of Acts is still being written as the Church still is performing the "acts" of the Holy Spirit.

Although we know that Paul was finally executed, the official history of the early Church ends on a positive note. No man can forbid the preaching of the gospel once God opens the door of spiritual opportunity! God can even block the opposition that comes from our own brothers and sisters in Christ. It is an unfortunate fact that so much of our energy is wasted because of the lack of unity in the Church. Instead of fighting our real enemy the devil, so many of God's people fight each other. However, an open spiritual door can also block the opposition that comes from within. Paul also experienced this in Acts 28:21, *And they said unto him. We neither received letters out of Judæa* (the center of Paul's opposition) *concernng thee...*

Therefore, it is obvious that what is needed throughout the whole world is for Christians to understand and enter into the third level of prayer: intercession.

Knock, and the door shall be opened!

As I stated before, we cannot be too distinctive in our dividing the three types of prayer. One can petition, commune and intercede in the same prayer time. It is hard to intercede without communion with Christ. Our petitions will be more effective by communion. Our intercession includes petitions, fellowship and communion. However, by understanding the three types of prayer, we can pray more effectively.

As new Christians, we approach prayer as the means by which we can receive from God. In time, we begin to mature and desire more. The newness of our experience is no longer as strong, so we may think we are slipping. What is actually happening is that we are being weaned spiritually from our infant formula and are being prepared for adult food. Then, we must enter into spiritual communion and fellowship with Christ, through the work of the Holy Spirit.

Once we have begun our personal relationship with Christ, we begin to feel what He feels. We can no longer allow things to continue as they are and we volunteer in the army of prayer. David prophesied, "Your people shall be volunteers in the day of Your power."

At Christian Center we are experiencing continuous revival in the church. We have volunteered to pray until the gospel is preached in the whole world. The doors will be opened as the spiritual forces are bound in the name of Jesus.

5

PRAYING IN THE SPIRIT

> ...*I will pray with the spirit, and I will pray with the understanding also; I will sing with the spirit, and I will sing with the understanding also.*
> I Corinthians 14:15

The most excited people I know speak in tongues.

The first time speaking in tongues was ever mentioned in the Bible was by Jesus Himself!

In the 16th chapter of Mark where Jesus was speaking to His disciples, He made some very emphatic statements of what He expected from the believers. He did not say tongues were just for the disciples or that generation. The Apostle Peter said in Acts 2:39, *For the promise is unto you, and to your children, and to all that are afar off, even as many as the Lord our God shall call.* As long as people are born into the world, men and women will receive the Holy Spirit with evidence of speaking in tongues.

TONGUES is a special spiritual gift, a divine endowment, a miraculous power given to the early Christians on the Day of Pentecost. If we could not benefit from praying in the Spirit, God would have never given this precious gift to us. Jesus Christ said in Mark 16:17, before He ascended into heaven, *And these signs shall follow them that believe; In my name shall they cast out devils; they shall speak with new tongues.*

I find that my prayer language is a great spiritual blessing to me. The more I use my prayer language the more I realize the tremendous importance of tongues in my own personal Christian life. I spend a good deal of my prayer life praying in my spiritual language. Like Paul, I pray in the spirit, and I pray with my understanding. In public, I would rather pray in a language which all can understand. The Scripture states in I Corinthians 14:2, *For he that speaketh in an unknown tongue speaketh not unto men, but unto God: for no man understandeth him; howbeit in the spirit he speaketh mysteries.*

Praying In The Spirit

I saw the power of the Holy Spirit operate in my oldest sister while she was still in her teens. She had a beautiful born-again experience, and prayed many weeks for the infilling of the Holy Spirit. When she spoke in tongues, she would be preaching. The pastor and church members marveled at the unusual moving of the Holy Spirit upon her life.

One Sunday a missionary from China visited our church. When the Christians gathered around the altar at the close of the service, the power of the Holy Spirit came upon Anna. She began preaching in the Chinese language. The missionary stopped praying and began to look for the one using their prayer language. He came to where mother was kneeling and said, "Sister, do you realize what is happening to your daughter? She has a call to China! There are many dialects in China, and your daughter has spoken the same dialect that I use in my ministry. In all my years of preaching I have never heard a more definite call. Your daughter gave a vivid description of the cross and the suffering of Christ for the sins of the whole world and the imminent return of Christ. She pleaded with them to repent in a flawless Chinese dialect. She told of her family, friends and home land she had left behind and expressed concern that they hear the gospel of Jesus Christ." Some people ask, can God speak through people today in a language they have never learned. I am glad He can and does—in spite of all men's teaching to the contrary.

This is entirely in accord with the Scriptures. On the day of Pentecost the hundred and twenty *were all filled with the Holy Ghost, and began to speak with other tongues, as the Spirit gave utterance* (Acts 2:4). There are some, however, who will not admit that on the day of Pentecost the disciples spoke in tongues they never had learned. They contend that the disciples simply grew excited and reverted to their native tongues. They do not contradict the fact that God caused the people to speak in new tongues at the tower of Babel, but they deny that He could make them speak with new tongues on the day of Pentecost! They claim that the disciples were from far countries, where other languages were spoken. The Bible plainly says that Christ chose His disciples as He went about His own country and the regions close by. At the time of Christ's ascension, after the disciples had watched Him go up out of their sight, the angel addressed them by saying, "Ye men of Galilee." And on the day of Pentecost those of the multitude which

Praying In The Spirit 67

gathered *were all amazed and marvelled, saying one to another, Behold, are not all these which speak Galilæans? And how hear we every man in our own tongue, wherein we were born!* (Acts 2:7-8).

Again in Acts 10:45-46 we read that Peter and other Jewish believers from Joppa were astonished *because that on the Gentiles also was poured out the gift of the Holy Ghost. For they heard them speak with tongues, and magnify God.* When the apostles at Jerusalem learned what had happened, they glorified God and rejoiced. They did not rejoice because the Gentiles had spoken in tongues; but they rejoiced because the Gentiles had been baptized with the Holy Spirit, and they knew this to be so because they had spoken with other tongues.

I am glad the Lord led my family into this Pentecostal experience. Mother found Christ in a Methodist Tent Revival when she was eighteen. Of course, she studied the Bible some, but she was well past thirty before she heard that people could received the baptism of the Holy Spirit and speak in tongues as the disciples did on the day of Pentecost.

Sometimes, I feel a burden of prayer; yet, I may not know exactly what I should pray for;

or, I may not have exactly the words to express what I feel. This is the time that I enter into my spiritual language and pierce through my natural ability to articulate to God what I am feeling. I go directly into my Father's presence in the Holy Spirit.

The baptism of the Holy Spirit is not just an experience, it's a relationship with God. Speaking in tongues is a reality. When I allowed the Holy Spirit to control my tongue, I find that my spirit is able to speak to God as I pray in tongues. The operations of the Holy Spirit and the gifts of the Holy Spirit are thrilling for us as we see the Body of Christ working together.

When I use my prayer language I can sense my faith actually being built as I pray in the Holy Spirit. The everyday, abiding, comforting presence of the Holy Spirit means the most to me; knowing that God's Holy Spirit dwells within me totally, comforting and maturing me as a person.

Mother often said, "The baptism of the Holy Spirit brought a whole new way of life to me." It was the opening of a new door in her life. God had to deal with her for some time in order to open her mind to His Word. When she began to pray for the baptism of the Holy Spirit with speaking in tongues, all those barriers that she had built up thru the years were swept away by the language of God's Spirit.

Since Mother was Pentecostal before I was born, I lived in an atmosphere of prayer and praise and my young life was open to the moving of the Holy Spirit. God began to reveal Himself to me early in my youth, just as He had revealed Himself to Mother in her youth. I would hear her pray in the Holy Spirit with tongues. To my father it all seemed strange and he really did not know what it was all about. I would become excited when I heard the manifestation of her singing in tongues. Although I could not understand any of the words, I loved it. Almost any time while she was having devotions I would stop playing and be very quiet, and begin to listen. I was thrilled when I would hear this beautiful singing in tongues. At a prayer meeting while others were praying in English, I heard Mother worshiping God in her prayer language.

I remember there were times when I was in bed with a fever, she would kneel by the bed, and lay her hand upon my head and begin to pray. She didn't pray in English! Words came out in her prayer language that I could not understand. it really did not matter what she was praying, for I knew when she stopped praying that within a few minutes, I would get up and be free from the fever and all aches and pain.

Now that I am a minister I know that it is important for my messages to build faith in the hearts of God's people. I spend a good deal of time bringing my own faith level up by praying in the Holy Spirit.

I meet many Christian's who have not used this important spiritual gift and I believe that the Holy Spirit today is calling all Christians to come closer together spiritually. It is my prayer that we may all agree and all see the importance of using the spiritual prayer language. I could not write a book or preach a sermon without honestly sharing with you that the Holy Spirit is a great spiritual help in prayer.

There is an internal struggle going on in the life of many Christians. The spirit is constantly warring against the flesh. By building yourself spiritually, you will find strength to overcome the flesh which is trying to drag you down.

Today, I received a phone call from a doctor. He was lamenting how weak he was and that he had determined many times not to fight with his wife, use bad language and do evil deeds. He said so often since he had become a Christian, he had tried to be kind but continued to fail. What could he do to strengthen himself spiritually? The answer I gave him was to develop his spiritual prayer language. When he learns how to pray in the Holy Spirit, this will cause him to be built up spiritually to the degree that he will be able to overcome all of the temptations of the flesh.

Romans 8:26, *Likewise the Spirit also helpeth our infirmities: for we know not what we should pray for as we ought: but the Spirit itself maketh intercession for us with groanings which cannot be uttered.*

Paul says that the Holy Spirit itself makes intercession for us! The way to be strengthened to help our infirmities is to pray in our prayer language. The Holy Spirit knows our spiritual need better than we do. However, He will use our own tongue to pray for our need. Praise the Lord for the Holy Spirit!

One Wednesday our family experienced an unusual event in prayer which illustrates what I am sharing with you. Mother locked the door to our house and we walked to the church where a prayer meeting was being held. As we returned home and were still several blocks from our house, she felt something was wrong. She was deeply burdened. There on the sidewalk she began to pray. Soon she stopped praying in her natural language, then went into her prayer language. After a time, the burden started to lift, and she knew that she had been heard and she had an answer.

When we arrived home, we found that our house had been broken into. The thief had strewn clothes all over the yard, on the porch and inside the house. Everything had been plundered. Yet, something strange had happened. Several pieces of antique jewelry were untouched. Somehow, the thief had been blinded to these things. He had only taken the men's clothing. We believe that when she was praying, the Holy Spirit showed her the need that caused her to pray. We feel that as the Holy Spirit was interceding through her the thief became frightened and rushed out of the house dropping part of his loot. Had we arrived while he was inside someone could have been harmed. God saw and God answered!

We were in Vietnam during the war and were invited to minister with Pa and Ma Kincade. They had rented a large house and each evening it was open to our American service men. It was a place to relax and enjoy a home cooked meal, have a Bible study and give testimonies of the tremendous miracles that happened while fighting in the jungles.

There were times they were in danger. Many of them would come and say, "Pastor Kincade, please pray for our buddies, we do not know the danger they may be facing." His response to them was, "Why don't we ask God to use our prayer language and pray through us for your buddies." They would pray, "Oh God, we do not know where they are. Neither do we know what conditions they are facing." Soon, we were all praying in our prayer language and we would continue to pray in the Spirit until the burden lifted. I testify to the glory of God that during the time we were in Vietnam, not one of our soldiers attending Bible study died. The bullets did fly around them, but our boys were protected by the Holy Spirit!

This is why I do not neglect the prayer language which God has graciously given me. I ask you to pray about this important form of prayer. Ask God to show you how you, too, can be protected, built up and strengthened by the Holy Spirit in a new way. For you who pray in the Holy Spirit, please do not quench the Spirit in your life!

I Thessalonians 5:18-21, *In every thing give thanks: for this is the will of God in Christ Jesus concerning you. Quench not the Spirit. Despise not prophesying. Prove all things; hold fast that which is good.*

To be a spiritual intercessor, we must have a desire to stand in prayer. "Intercessor" literally means to stand between. We must be willing to stand between the need and God, the only one able to meet the need. We must also be willing to be used by the Holy Spirit in prayer at unexpected times and in unexpected places. We must be willing to be used by the Holy Spirit to pray for needs that we are not aware of naturally. The need may be in another part of the world. When my brother was in South America, I was awakened by the Holy Spirit to pray for his safety. I learned later he was going through a jungle infested with wild beasts and snakes. The Holy Spirit desired to use me to meet that need in prayer. God is looking for people who are willing to be used by Him.

God wants the gifts of the Spirit to operate in the Body. When we gather in His name, He wants each one of us to contribute to the service in some way—by singing a psalm, or teaching, or bringing a message in another tongue, or by interpreting such a message, or by prophesying, or telling of a spiritual revelation, or speaking words of exhortation and comfort one to another. If people are required to hold fast to a previously-arranged order of service, how can the Spirit of God move in the Body and bring forth that which He wills?

Why should we speak in tongues when we are baptized with the Holy Spirit? Because there is a wave of glory that sweeps over our souls and bodies when we receive this glorious experience. That is why we sing, "it is joy unspeakable and full of glory." Paul testified in I Corinthians 14:18, *I thank my God, I speak with tongues more than ye all.* This he spoke to a church he was correcting on the overuse of spiritual manifestations.

There are so many wonderful facts and features of the baptism of the Holy Spirit, which I fear are neglected in our preaching today. We have a "treasure" (II Corinthians 4:7) in these earthen vessels. A very "good thing" (II Timothy 1:14) has been committed to us in the Holy Ghost. May God give us a proper appreciation of the fullness of the blessing of the gospel of Christ.

In I Corinthians 14 we have some very clear teaching concerning the gift of tongues, the gift of the interpretation of tongues and the gift of prophecy. If we speak in an unknown tongue, we should pray that we may interpret. On the other hand, the Word says, "Forbid not to speak with tongues." It also says, "Covet to prophesy," for prophecy does not need to be interpreted.

There is prayer in an unknown tongue, and prayer with the understanding. There is singing with the spirit, and there is singing with the understanding also.

When I was a small child, I heard songs that were given by the Spirit. Holy Spirit-filled saints sang them in the service in tongues and the Lord gave the interpretation of the words. These songs are what Paul calls, in Ephesians 5:19, "spiritual songs." We rejoice in the Lord that He has given such marvelous gifts to His people; yet we, like Paul, would rather testify to some lost soul and lead him to Christ than to do any amount of speaking in tongues.

Oh, if you have not received this glorious Pentecostal baptism, you are missing the best thing the Lord has for His born-again people this side of heaven. He will give you this infilling of the Holy Spirit if you will ask Him for it. The promise is, *If ye then, being evil, know how to give good gifts unto your children, how much more shall your Father which is in heaven give good things to them that ask him?* (Matt. 7:11).

I am glad the Lord led my family into this Pentecostal experience of the bapatism of the Holy Spirit and speaking in tongues, as the disciples did on the day of Pentecost.

6

PRAYER CREATES FAITH

But without faith it is impossible to please him: For he that cometh to God must believe that he is, and that he is a rewarder of them that diligently seek him.
Hebrews 11:6

Faith has to do with all the vital issues of the Christian experience. That means every day we should live by faith.

Romans 1:17, *For therein is the righteousness of God revealed from faith to faith: as it is written, The just shall live by faith.*

In other words, when we come to God in prayer, we must come in an attitude of faith. God does not make faith in prayer optional. We must have faith in prayer in order for our prayer to be heard. Therefore, God will not hear prayer that is in doubt. He will only hear prayers that are in faith!

You ask how can we develop the prayer of faith?

Our faith must be clearly directed toward a goal! Just as a bullet fired from a gun is set on a definite target, so also our prayers of faith must be set on a definite target. People often ask me, "Please pray that the Lord will bless me." My response is, "What kind of blessing do you want? There are thousands of blessings in the Bible. You must be specific in order to get an answer, otherwise how will you know when God has answered you?"

If you have a financial need, do not just ask God, "Lord, I need a special amount for a new set of tires, and I am asking you to please send me this amount so that I may pay for the tires so that no shame may come to your servant because of a flat tire." If you need tires ask for that amount specifically! If you need a new car, do not ask for tires, ask for the amount you need for a car!

We were pastors of the New Life Temple in Hong Kong. While one 11 a.m. Sunday morning service was in progress, a lady walked to the platform and talked to my husband. Before his message he made the announcement that in the afternoon at 2 p.m. he would conduct a funeral for one of our Christian brothers. His wife was a Buddhist. She phoned to ask that we pray that "our God" would stop the rain. It was the rainy season and they have torrential rains during that time of the year. The Chinese feel it is a bad omen if it rains during a funeral. We knew it would have to be a miracle for the rain to stop. The audience stood and prayed with my husband for God to stop the rain. By 12 noon the sun was shining. It continued shining until after the funeral. As we were leaving the cemetery, dark clouds began to gather in the sky. Large drops of rain began to fall. Before we reached home we had a downpour.

The next day the little widow sent for us. She said, "My husband was a Christian. He tried many times to show me that Buddha never gave me a miracle. He said, 'Christians have miracles!!' Before telephoning the church, I prayed all morning asking Buddha to stop the rain. It only rained harder. When I called for prayer and the rain stopped I knew it had to be a miracle. I know that your God is the true God. Now, I want to become a Christian and

Prayer Creates Faith

I want to be baptized in water. Pastor, I want you to baptize me." We could see that her legs were crippled from arthritis. She asked if the bath tub would be okay. I did not think we could get her in the tub. We told her that we would be back tomorrow.

We talked to the Chinese Christians. One lady came up with the idea that since it would be almost impossible to get her in a tub, she had a beautiful silver bowl which we could use to baptize the widow by sprinkling. We practice emersion, but due to this lady's physical condition, we would do the next best thing. We had quite a little group who went along. My husband explained that due to her badly crippled condition he would sprinkle her in the "Name of the Father, Son and Holy Spirit." It was a thrilling experience. She smiled and told her interpreter she wanted to speak to the Pastor. She spoke through an interpreter, who in turn spoke through another interpreter, who interpreted her words in English! With a beautiful smile on her face, patting her chest she said, "I am so happy, I am no longer a worshiper of Buddha. I know that Jesus Christ is the true God. Now, I can meet my husband in heaven."

God has always responded to direct and

specific prayers. Everything He does has a plan and purpose. In Genesis 1 and 2, we are told that God created within specific time frames called days. When He told Moses to build a Tabernacle, He gave him clear directions. Moses was not left to decide whether he would build the tent around twenty cubits long; no, he was told exactly how long and how wide. Therefore, God is a precise God and He expects us to pray precisely! Faith is the substance of things! Faith is not the substance of generalities, but of definite things hoped for. And faith is the evidence of things hoped for—again very specific (see Hebrews 11:1).

The prayer of faith will lead us into visions and dreams! The prophet Joel said in Joel 2:28, *And it shall come to pass afterward, that I will pour out my spirit upon all flesh; and your sons and your daughters shall prophesy, your old men shall dream dreams, your young men shall see visions.* How do the young see visions and the old dream dreams? They are able to do so because visions and dreams are the language of the Holy Spirit. When referring to the faith of Abraham, Paul said in Romans 4:17, *. . .before him whom he believed, even God, who quickeneth the dead, and calleth those things which be not as though they were.*

Prayer Creates Faith

Abraham's faith was amplified in Romans not only describing the nature of Abraham's faith, but also the nature of his God on whom his faith rested. God was able to create and impart a vision and a dream concerning His vious to the eye was, by faith, still real. Therefore, Abraham "staggered not" at the promise of God. Because God said it, Abraham believed, not looking at his own physical incapability to produce an offspring at the age of one hundred years. Abraham had the reality of his visions and dreams.

So it is in prayer, that is the prayer of faith, that we must learn to visualize the results before God brings them, calling those things which are not as if they were. If you long for a child to bring happiness to your childless home, then begin to see that child in your visions and dreams. You and your husband should not only pray and ask for the child, but begin to see a new baby boy or girl, bright and healthy, filling your home with happiness. At night, fill your heart with that dream. In the morning, let that be your vision. Just as Abraham and Sarah were able to see their child by faith, not counting the fact that both were way beyone the childbearing stage of life, you too, can see the child of your faith-prayer come into being.

Abraham was told to look at the stars and count them at night. So would his offspring be in number. His imagination was overwhelmed with the fulfillment of his faith. He was filled with God's promise. In the day Abraham was told to get on top of a mountain and look to the east, north, south and west, he was promised that everything he could see would be his possession. His imagination was again filled with God's promise. His vision was used by God to build faith.

Man still knows little about how his mind and body works. Man knows even less about his spirit. Visualization is being spoken by man as a new discovery, but God has revealed this principle throughout the entire Scripture. God has promised to give us the desires of our heart. Prayer is petition, but our desires must be in line with the Word of God, the Bible! For example, I knew a Christian girl who prayed for a young man to marry. She met a man who was not a Christian, and she thought that man was the answer to her prayer. After having counseling sessions for two years she said, "Why can't we get married?" The Bible says in II Corinthians 6:14, *Be ye not unequally yoked together with unbelievers: for what fellowsip hath righteousness with unrighteousness? and what communion hath light with darkness?* I told her no matter how she prayed for that young man to be her husband, the Word of God has dictated the fact that God will not honor this relationship. She may pray specifically; she may use visions and dreams in her imagination; she may claim all of the promises; but God only responds to those prayers in accordance with the revealed Word of God, the Bible! I received a letter from her in the past two weeks telling me that she decided to break the engagement and she planned to attend Oral Roberts University.

God is the God of the eternal now! He sees the end from the beginning. The faith that God responds to is the "now" faith mentioned in the first verse of Hebrews 11. When we pray in faith we move into God's fourth dimensional realm of "now" faith. We see the results of God's promise to us as already done. We do not faint because of the circumstances which might seem impossible, but we come into the rest of God. That is, we stand firm, not wavering, knowing that God is faithful to do exceedingly, abundantly more that we can ask or think. Do not put off God's answer into the future, "Someday God will answer me!" We must call those things which be not as though they were. Abram's name was changed to Abraham (father of many) before his first son was born by his wife Sarah. Can you imagine the reaction of all who knew this powerful man? They must have shaken their heads, wondering why this old man would change his name without having the results of his promise. Yet Abraham's faith did not waiver. He had learned to move into the "now" faith of God and call those things which were not as though they were already.

Abraham is called the father of faith because he experienced dynamic faith which has become an example for us all. Romans 4:23-24, *Now, it was not written for his* (Abraham's) *sake alone, that it* (faith) *was imputed to him; but for us also, . . .* We must learn from Abraham, in learning the prayer of faith!

Finally, to pray in faith, we must remove all obstacles that may hinder God's answer!

The prayer of faith requires us to continue praying until we have the assurance in our hearts that God has heard us and the answer is on its way. Romans 10:17, *So then faith cometh by hearing, and hearing by the word of God.* Faith is released when we pray. If we stop praying before that assurance comes, then we may not have generated sufficient faith to get our prayer answered.

We must also watch our confession! In the ninth verse of Romans 10, confession is linked to faith. So often, Christians loose the answer to their prayers because they begin to confess negative statements. "I prayed, but I do not think God will do it!" Never try to work on God's pity by your negative confession. God does not respond to pity, but He does respond to faith. God cannot be manipulated by selfpity. "Nobody seems to care about me!" or "I know I will be ruined!" Clear out all of the self-pity and begin to move in faith! Your attitude may determine the level of faith in which you pray. If your confession is negative, it reveals that your heart is also negative! For out of our hearts our mouths speak.

A positive confession will cause you to praise God for the answer, even before you see it! You will wake up in the morning knowing that God has heard you and you will confess with your mouth praise and thanksgiving. This will build your faith and will cause the hand of God to move on your behalf.

We must clear all of the sin out of our lives to move in the prayer of faith!

I John 3:21-22, *Beloved, If our heart condemn us not, then have we confidence toward God. And whatsoever we ask, we receive of him, because we keep his commandments, and do those things that are pleasing in his sight.*

If you have sin in your life, confess it to the Father today! Do not wait until the morning! Do it now! Cleanse your heart before God so that there might be a clear channel of prayer between you and your heavenly Father.

I John 1:9, *If we confess our sins, he is faithful and just to forgive us our sins, and to cleanse us from all unrighteousness.*

You can keep every obstacle of sin, bitterness, hatred or fear from blocking the measure of faith that God has given to us. That measure of faith can grow and develop so that we may pray in faith. Now is the time to begin to pray in faith! The results of this kind of prayer will be miraculous: James 5:15, *And the prayer of faith shall save the sick, and the Lord shall raise him up; and if he have committed sins, they shall be forgiven him.*

Consider the plight of a blind man (Mark 10:46-52). Put yourself in his place. He longed to enjoy life as others. The man's condition had caused him to be separated from society. He had to sit by the wayside, begging for the portions usually handed to the blind. At night, he had to find his way back home and prepare a meal for himself as best he could. Day after day he sat and begged. The people dodged him; the religionists drew in their cloaks as they passed him by, ostentatiously flipping in a farthing or a mite. They did not care about him; he was just a blind beggar.

But, that man had a precious soul that was crying out for deliverance. He had heard that Jesus of Nazareth, who healed the blind, was passing by. As Jesus came near, he could feel the presence of a power greater than any he had ever known, and he cried out, "Jesus!" From his heart he was crying to the Savior. "Have mercy on me! I know I am not worthy. I am just a poor, blind beggar. But, Jesus, please do not pass me by. I need deliverance." Our Savior will never reject such a plea.

This same Jesus is before you at this moment. He is there now in the room with you as you read this message. He is standing by your side. The Lord does not look upon you with eyes of condemnation; He looks upon you with love. No matter who you are or where you are from, the Lord Jesus Christ loves you. He wants to reveal Himself to you as your Savior and your healer.

What did Jesus do next? The Word of God tells us that He turned toward His followers and told them to bring the blind man to Him. Friend, as this was His command to His followers then, this is also the command of Jesus Christ to His followers today. The call of Jesus Christ to His Church is to bring the halt, the lame, and the blind to Him. He commands ministers to bring deliverance to the suffering multitudes today. If they reject His command, they are sinning against the Lord and the people.

THE HEALING CHRIST

As He commanded, they called the blind man, saying, *Be of good comfort, rise; he calleth for thee* (Mark 10:49). Jesus did not go to him; He stood and waited. Now the responsibility was Bartimaeus'. If he had remained beside the highway he would not have been healed, even though Jesus waited. Bartimæus had to act by faith.

The Word of God tells us that *he, casting away his garment, rose, and came to Jesus* (Mark 10:50). He threw off his beggar's robe, leaped to his feet, and stood before the Master. The robe the beggars wore signified their position in life. The robe represented his past life.

By faith he said, "I won't need this anymore." He left his past and entered a new future with Christ. This was the act of faith that put his old life behind him. Then, coming to Jesus, he found the contact with God that brought his healing.

Some ask, "If there is such an abundant provision for our salvation and healing, why is there so much sin and sickness?" I'll tell you why. You must take a step toward Him. Jesus Christ will not force anyone to come. He is waiting, but you must come to Him. Now is the time to act. His provisions for your need is available. The Lord Jesus Christ wants you to take that beggar's robe off. Then He will open your eyes; He will heal your cancer, heart trouble, arthritis, or any other disease.

When Bartimæus stood before Him, Jesus said, *What wilt thou that I should do unto thee?* He said, *Lord, that I might receive my sight.* (Mark 10:51). The Lord commanded the blindness to leave, and immediately the miracle took place. The man was no longer blind, physically or spiritually. He did not put on his beggar's robe, nor return to his former ways. The Bible tells us that he followed Jesus in the way, proclaiming His power.

THE SAVING CHRIST

You may not be a blind beggar like Bartimæus, but all of us stand in need of the power of Christ. Many spend their lives separated from all that is good, simply because they will not throw away their beggar's garment and surrender to Christ. The only way to have peace, joy, and happiness is to follow Jesus Christ every day of your life.

When the Lord opened Bartimaeus' eyes, he knew he was healed. He did not doubt what had taken place. So it is when you are saved. You know when the Lord opens your eyes spiritually. You know when you pass from darkness to light. Some say, "I go to church. I pay money to the church." That does not save you. To be saved is to know that you are born again. Jesus said, *Ye must be born again* (John 3:7). The Lord will break the fetters that bind; He will dispel the darkness from your life; He will deliver you; He will enable you to walk in the light as He is in the light. Why grope in the darkness when you may see clearly, when you may know where you are going?

Bartimæus had to let the supernatural power of Jesus Christ come into his life. If you could have saved yourself, God would not have sent His Son to Calvary. Jesus came because our deliverance had to be a supernatural deliverance. You can be saved only as you open your heart to Jesus and let Him come in. There is no other way. The supernatural work of Christ is all that will change a man's nature completely. *If any man be in Christ, he is a new creature.* Christ will take away your old life of sin and you will say, *Behold, all things are become new* (II Corinthians 5:17).

Christ paid the price on Calvary's cross that you might have life forevermore. He is now beckoning you to come to Him. He took the stripes on His back for your healing. You can be healed right now. You can also know that you are saved—you need not go on wondering. Jesus said, *Him that cometh to me I will in no wise cast out* (John 6:37). He is calling you NOW!

7

PRAYER AND FASTING

Sanctify ye a fast, call a solemn assembly, gather the elders and all the inhabitants of the land into the house of the LORD your God, and cry unto the LORD.
Joel 1:14

Fasting is abstinence from food for the purpose of prayer. Fasting and praying can break the band of wickedness and cause the oppressed to go free; and bring total and complete deliverance.

Jesus performed a miracle in Matthew 17:14-21. The Bible records the time when the Lord's disciples were unable to cast an evil spirit out of a boy. The child's father said to Jesus, *Lord, have mercy on my son: for he is lunatic,. . .ofttimes he falleth into the fire. . .and I brought him to thy disciples, and they could not cure him* (Matthew 17:15-16).

Can you imagine the disciples' frustration as they gathered around the boy who tossed and writhed uncontrollably on the ground? They had prayed and rebuked the devil over and over again, but nothing had happened.

Then Jesus came and . . .*rebuked the devil; and he departed out of him: and the child was cured from that very hour. Then came the disciples to Jesus apart, and said, Why could not we cast him* (the evil spirit) *out? And Jesus said unto them, Because of your unbelief: for verily I say unto you, If ye have faith as a grain of mustard seed, ye shall say unto this mountain, Remove hence to yonder place; and it shall remove; and nothing shall be impossible unto you. Howbeit this kind goeth not out but by prayer and fasting* (Matthew 17:18-21). Only prayer and fasting could bring deliverance to the child. In difficult cases, you are wise to combine fasting with prayer. Fasting means to deny yourself not only of food but pleasures and distractions.

God is calling the Body of Christ to become active in prayer and fasting and to call on Him to pour out great, and unusual manifestations of His power. God is about to bring forth a great deluge of His power. It will be the greatest move of the Spirit of God in the history of the human race. Think about it! We are going to have the glorious privilege of not only witnessing the move of God's Spirit in these last days, but also being the vessels through which this mighty power will flow!

Christians need to concentrate on the importance of fasting and prayer in connection with the outpouring of God's Spirit.

Let's go back to the scripture in Joel 2. Before the Spirit of God is poured out upon all flesh, verse 12 says, *Turn ye even to me with all your heart, and with fasting, and with weeping, and with mourning.* Mourning was an old covenant figure of speech which described the prophets taking the sin of a whole nation on their shoulders and interceding, crying out to God until it was lifted.

Have you wondered why you could not cast out a devil? There are battles to be won that can only be won by prayer.

A few months ago, a demon possessed girl came to South Bend from Denver, Colorado. This family was not concerned with the physical difficulties involved in bringing her the hundreds of miles they had to travel. Their one desire was that their demon possessed daughter be set free. She was a beautiful young lady, twenty-four years of age, who was tormented by Satan. She kicked and screamed each mile of the trip. In the natural, deliverance seemed impossible, but the father, who stood strong in faith, assured his family that through God all things were possible.

When the family arrived the father said, "I am determined to stay until my daughter is delivered from the power of the devil."

The first day we dealt with the young lady there was no visible sign of healing. When we met the second day, we felt the strength of God's Spirit, but still there was very little change in the girl's condition. At times, she would become violent. Threatening to kill us, we didn't give up, but continued to take authority over the power of Satan. When we met on the third day, she stopped cursing and fighting. After praying for three hours the girl suddenly cried out, "Oh my God, please help me! Will someone help?" Her body became stiff, her facial expression was one of pain. Tears ran down her face as she continued pleading for help. Each intercessor began taking authority over the devil. It was a strong spirit. She grabbed her side saying, "These claws are killing me." She tried to stand, but did not have the strength and fell to the floor. Then she grabbed her shoulder and neck saying, "His claws are tearing into my shoulder, Oh God!" she cried, "The pain is more than I can bear." Then she fainted. When she became conscious, the men helped her onto a chair. From this attack her body became weak. We saw that she needed rest. We advised her parents to take her to the motel and bring her back the next morning.

The next morning she told us of her involvement in witchcraft and spiritism. She said, "I am further possessed through dope and alcohol. I lived with a young Mexican boy who was able to control my mind." As she began to cry her body shook. She said, "I want deliverance." We began to pray. This was to be the final surge that would break Satan's power. Everyone in the room seemed to have a new anointing of the Holy Spirit. She jumped to her feet and cried, "I am free! I am free! I am free!

They attended Thursday night meeting. We had a baptismal service. As the minister was leaving the tank, she ran to the pastor and asked, "Can I be baptized?" You should have seen the shine on her face as she came out of the baptismal tank.

Prayer And Fasting

The following day the family returned to Denver. The father telephoned back to the church. They made the trip home with no problem and were still rejoicing over the deliverance God had given their daughter.

There are victories that are ours, but they are ours only through prayer. Some things you can do if you want to, but for some things you need reinforcement.

The moment you begin to pray, you enter into conflict with the dark forces of the spirit world. Remember that Paul says, . . .*we wrestle not against flesh and blood, but against principalities, against powers, against the rulers of the darkness of this world, against spiritual wickedness in high places (Ephesians 6:12).* Fasting will give more power to your prayers. It will help you to be more alert spiritually because your heart, soul, and body will be totally focused upon God.

Prayer and fasting are sources of strength and deliverance and that is why we urge all Christians to make a new prayer commitment before God.

In I Corinthians 7:5 it says, *Defraud ye not one the other, except it be with consent for a time, that ye may give yourselves to fasting and prayer; and come together again, that Satan tempt you not for your incontinency.* There is a time when we can remove ourselves from the normal, natural duties of a home, even of a husband and wife, and separate ourselves for a time of tremendous fasting and prayer when we literally give ourselves to prayer. Now that has not happened to many people. The prayer life of most Christians consists of "Good morning, Jesus" and about twelve hours later "Good night, Lord," and over the food, "Lord, you know we're thankful," and that's about it. The whole thing could be done in about two minutes. That is not what we're talking about. We are speaking of using prayer as an awesome force, a tremendous power, a world-changing influence—and it is the greatest source of untapped energy in the world.

If enough of us change our prayer habits and our thought habits regarding prayer, we can see the Church of Jesus Christ change in America and in the rest of the world. God is no respecter of persons, whether it is in the Philippines, Japan, the Isles of the Sea, or South America. You can receive the power of God that you will not receive from any other source.

Acts 10:2 describes Cornelius as being a devout man and one that feared God, with all of his house, and he prayed always and gave much alms. Your family praying with you strengthens your prayers; if one can chase a thousand, the Bible says two can put ten thousand to flight. Your home united in prayer is like an army ready to go to battle.

God responded with miracles. He said, "Listen, I have a man named Simon Peter who is a hundred miles away in another town, over in Joppa. I will send him to your own town of Cæsarea and things will begin to happen." While Peter was yet preaching, Cornelius and his whole family received the infilling of the Holy Spirit, but the beginning of these things was prayer. Too many of us think that miracles come haphazardly, but this is not true. Through the instrument and power and the authority of prayer we can receive tremendous things from God that could never be received any other way. You can be remembered as a person who changed today's world and the next world—through the power of prayer.

In II Corinthians 1:11 it reads, *Ye also helping together by prayer for us, that for the gift bestowed upon us by the means of many persons thanks may be given by many on our behalf.* Prayer is not a selfish thing. You can help your neighbor through prayer; you can help the missionaries through prayer; you can help your minister through prayer. It is a building up of energy to be released.

Prayer will release energy and blessing that we have never known before.

Acts 12:5 says, *Peter therefore was kept in prison: but prayer was made without ceasing of the church unto God for him.* No wonder the prison doors had to open. Prayers commanded God and God commanded the angel and Peter was set free by the power of God.

By prayer and fasting we release God's power in our lives. We can move into a tremendous reservoir of energy that you and I and the rest of the Church have not used in our generation?

The Holy Spirit will aid us in our prayer. *Likewise the Spirit also helpeth our infirmities: for we know not what we should pray for as we ought: but the Spirit itself maketh intercession for us* (Romans 8:26). You have a partner in prayer. You are not alone. You can pray by the anointing and unction of the Holy Spirit, and through Him you will have prayers answered that could never have come to you otherwise.

In public gatherings, the early Church fasted and prayed in order to know the will of God. In Acts 13, the Holy Spirit was able to clearly direct the church: *Now there were in the church that was at Antioch certain prophets and teachers; as Barnabas, and Simeon that was called Niger, and Lucius of Cyrene, and Manaen, which had been brought up with Herod the tetrarch, and Saul. As they ministered to the Lord, and fasted, the Holy Ghost said, Separate me Barnabas and Saul for the work whereunto I have called them. And when they had fasted and prayed...they sent them away.* (Acts 13:1-3).

And whatsoever ye shall ask in my name, that will I do, that the Father may be glorified in the Son. (John 14:13). The scope of prayer is as large as our asking. A life planned on the knees is a great life. Prayer will stamp an indelible mark on your every action and thought. It is a spiritual magnetism; like a magnet draws a piece of iron, prayer draws God, prayer draws men, and prayer draws conditions.

PRAYER AND FASTING IS A POWER THAT CANNOT BE DEFEATED. Nobody can stop it, although they have tried in every great empire. It is an invincible force. The act of praying and fasting generates omnipotence. It gives a frail human being an unshakable strength that he has never known before. Systems change, balances of power in the world change, balances of economics change, but prayer is a strength and a power that simply cannot be defeated.

At Christian Center Cathedral of Praise, we have men and women come from all parts of America to receive spiritual help. By fasting and prayer, the intercessor becomes aware of the urgency of the request. When the prayer request is known, the intercessors begin praying and fasting. These are Christians who have committed themselves to the ministry of INTERCESSION. Prayer continues daily until we know in our hearts that God has answered.

Jesus fasted and prayed 40 days in the wilderness before He began His ministry. Notice Matthew 4:1, *Then was Jesus led up by the Spirit into the wilderness to be tempted by the devil.* Before launching into a period of protracted fasting, be sure you are being led by the Holy Spirit. Some people fast because they think it is a good way to lose weight or to show others how religious they are.

My brother Lester asked Mother and me to come for a two week revival, while he and his wife attended an out of town convention.

From the beginning, the meetings were well attended. While praying, the Lord revealed that I should fast and pray three days. By the end of third day my body felt weak. God impressed me to preach on "The Demoniac of Gadara."

While preaching the anointing of the Holy Spirit came upon me in an unusual way. I told the audience the power of God was there to set men and women free from demon power, and that deliverance was available as when Jesus walked upon the earth. A woman called out from the back, "You cannot set me free!" I said, "Oh, yes we can. In the Name of Jesus you will be set free by the power of His blood. You will come out."

She walked up the aisle; her face was distorted. One could see Satan had really played havoc with her life. When she reached the altar, Walter G...was nearby and I asked him to pray with her. When he went over and began to pray, she pulled his hair and tried to fight. Then I asked Mother to pray with the lady. She prayed, but with no result. The Holy Spirit spoke to me. "Why have you been fasting the past three days?" I said, "Lord, I want power to set people free from Satan and I want God to give a great revival." He said, "I have given you the anointing. Go deliver the lady. So I went to where she was kneeling. She pretended to be praying and was saying words we could not understand. Then she began to speak in tongues. I recognized it as satanic. I screamed at the devil, and said, "You are trying to imitate the Holy Spirit. Don't you speak again!" She tried again. I said, "I demand you to stop!" I looked around. The Christians were shouting and praising God. They thought she had received the Holy Spirit. I said, "Friends, if you do not know the real power of God from the counterfeit, it might be better to go home. This woman spoke through the power of Satan; it was not by the power of the Holy Spirit." I bowed my head to pray and when I looked up almost everyone was gone. Only a few stayed, but they were ready for battle.

When we began to move with the authority of the Holy Spirit over the devil, she began to fight and curse. I demanded Satan to stop his cursing and using foul unclean words. The filth flowed from her lips. It was shocking. I demanded the unclean spirit to shut up. Then Satan changed and put on a religious act and she pretended to be praying. I knew it was not genuine; it was the wrong kind of prayer. She said, "The man in the back I was sitting with is not a wicked man. It is true he has many lovers, tells lies, and curses. Do you think he needs to get saved?" I said, "That is none of your business what he needs. What you need is to get your own life straightened out." When the man saw the people turn to look at him, he took his hat and left. Satan does not like to be identified. When he left, the spirit in the woman cried out saying, "Do not leave me." As Satan began to get stronger and stronger we took more authority over him. When she kept trying to speak I told Satan, "Shut up! We do not want to hear anything you have to say. You are filled with lies and you have been a liar from the beginning. I demand you shut up. In the name of Jesus, come out." I knew God would give us power and strength to deliver the woman. With a strong voice, I said, "Satan, I come against you by the power of the blood." She fell over and said, "I am dying." When I looked at her pale face, she looked dead.

Then Satan attacked with fear. He said, "See what you have done! How will you feel when your brother returns and he reads the headline in the daily newspaper. 'Woman dies in tent revival!!! Pastor Lester Sumrall was out of town. Visiting South Bend, his sister, Evangelist Leona Sumrall was casting a devil out of a woman when she collapsed and died during the session.' "

I cried, "Oh,.. .God." The Holy Spirit sweetly spoke to me. "The victory is almost won!" God gave me the assurance she would be delivered. We picked her up and sat her down in a chair. I was angry with the devil and commanded him to come out. She began to fight. I said, "You keep still, and Mr. Devil, you are finished and you are coming out." We had a battle for a few minutes. She began to say, "I am Alma." I said, "You are a lying spirit, and you are defeated." This was the last struggle. Color began to return to her face. She opened her eyes and smiled; tears streamed down her face. She began to praise God saying, "I am delivered from the bondage of the devil. I feel so clean." She seemed taller and very beautiful. She looked years younger as she left the tent.

It took fasting and prayer to break the stronghold of Satan.

As a result of the fast, several wonderful things happened. God gave me a new anointing in my ministry. There was no more fear. My calling as an evangelist was more anointed; my spirit became more sensitive to the leading of the Holy Spirit. From that time I have been alive to the will of God. God was present in power throughout that revival. Many, many people came to receive Jesus Christ as their Savior, and God performed miracles of healing in lives. Believe me when I say there is real

Prayer And Fasting

power in fasting. There is a reason for the emphasis on this form of self-discipline. Fasting is a constant reminder to your body that your spirit is going to be boss, that your spiritual hunger will prevail over your fleshly desire. Fasting is also a reminder to pray. When you feel hungry, use that sharp hunger pain as an alarm clock to arouse you to pray even more earnestly.

Throughout my ministry, God has led me to add power to my prayers through fasting. In a difficult situation, a three-day fast will add a new dimension to your prayers. (I would add that if there is a possibility that three days without nourishment could threaten your health, you would be wise to check with your doctor to see if a fast would be harmful.)

To the natural man, the idea of fasting sounds foolish. However, the Bible reveals that DESIRE IS THE KEY TO POWER WITH GOD!

Isaiah 64:7 really speaks to my heart. The prophet said to God, *There is none that calleth upon thy name, that stirreth up himself to take hold of thee...* Everyone was to lazy, too easygoing, too content to just let things slide along as usual. Powerful praying is hard work, and it requires extra effort from those who want to succeed in working for God and helping others. However, you will never make this great effort without a strong desire!

Jesus said, *Blessed are they which do hunger and thirst after righteousness: for they shall be filled (Matthew 5:6).* You will be spiritually fed.

8

PRAYER BRINGS REVIVAL

Wilt thou not revive us again: that thy people may rejoice in thee?
Psalm 85:6

O LORD, I have heard thy speech, and was afraid: O LORD, revive thy work in the midst of the years, in the midst of the years make known; in wrath remember mercy.
Habakkuk 3:2

What is revival? Revival is a spiritual awakening in the Body of Christ, an extraordinary move of the Holy Spirit which produces extraordinary results, an exciting and abiding relationship of Christ with people of many denominations. Revival is also the renewal of the first love of Christians.

Let us join in earnest prayer that God will give us a spiritual revival that brings an awareness of the holiness of God, a passion for lost souls that will motivate us to be about the Father's business, and discipleship that is clothed with servanthood.

One secret of the Pentecostal revival early in this century was the heartfelt reaching out to God in prayer by hundreds of people. All of us remember great answers to prayer in our Christian pilgrimage. One is the prayer for forgiveness. Another may be for the infilling of the Holy Spirit and the healing of the body, prayers for our faith and glory to the name of Jesus.

But, here is a prayer we should be praying as one voice in quiet desperation, *Wilt thou not revive us again: that thy people may rejoice in thee?* (Habakkuk 3:2).

Revivals affect history and nations. Peter's Pentecost wrote more history than Cæsar's conquests. Paul's Damascus road decision altered the face and destiny of the world in the first century more than any battle fought.

In true revival the work is never superficial, the mortar is never untempered, the materials never cheap and shoddy. Emotion and sentiment are never substituted for the presence and conviction of the Holy Spirit. There is no substitute for a real work of God. Christians stop doing what they should not do. Prayer breaks the power of the world and of sin over Christians.

Revival can neither be manufactured nor manipulated; it is the work of God. We cannot solve matters by depending upon the arm of the flesh. Conducting conferences and appointing committees cannot of themselves bring the desired results. Nothing can take the place of seeking God. It is far easier to get people to serve on committees, to be busy doing, than it is to get them to pray. Historic evidence indicates that revival is preceded with a wave of prayer. Too many Christians live on the overflow of others and their experiences slip into substitutionary spirituality.

Another concern is to see people accept Christ and then fail to let Him be Lord. Their commitment to His Lordship is lacking. Their lifestyle is not subject to His direction. There is little desire for prayer and the Word of God. Passion to win the lost is not evident. To be a follower of Christ is a great honor— the greatest one can receive. To really follow Him involves discipleship, and true discipleship is more than enjoying a spiritual high on Sunday mornings.

We can be concerned with building correct altars, rearranging the stones, and laying the sacrifice properly, and then fail to call down the fire. God give us Elijahs with prophetic ministries. Spiritual dearth will result in death. Just as we know that fire burns and that ice is cold, we know that a spiritual awakening is the answer to the needs of our world.

Isaiah recorded his life-changing confrontation with God: *. . .I saw also the Lord sitting upon a throne, high and lifted up, and his train filled the temple. Above it stood the seraphims. . .And one cried unto another, and said, Holy, holy, holy, is the LORD of hosts: the whole earth is full of his glory. And the posts of the door moved at the voice of him that cried, and the house was filled with smoke* (Isaiah 6:1-4).

We need to discover the height of God's unapproachable majesty, and His presence. He is almighty God, majestic and holy. A sense of the holiness and majesty of God can do for us what it did for Isaiah. He sensed his total inability, even more, his sinfulness. Hear him cry, *Woe is me! for I am undone; because I am a man of unclean lips, and I dwell in the midst of a people of unclean lips: for mine eyes have seen the King, the LORD of hosts* (Isaiah 6:5).

Isaiah then recorded that one of the seraphim took a live coal from the altar and laying it upon the prophet's mouth said, Lo, this hath touched thy lips; and thine iniquity is taken away, and thy sin purged (Isaiah 6:7).

With a God-given sense of His holiness we will not be asking, "What is wrong with this or that?" and, "Is it right to do thus and so?" Rather, we will ask, "What is this activity doing to my relationship with my Lord?" The right relationship to God not only brings the sense of His majesty and His holiness, but also His matchless love. We discover not only the height of His unapproachable majesty, but also the depths of His love for sinners.

Isaiah heard *the voice of the LORD, saying, Whom shall I send, and who will go for us? Then said I, Here am I; send me* (Isaiah 6:8).

Have you answered, "Here am I; send me."? Every Christian has a God-given task to tell the good news. Jesus said that just as it was necessary for Him to die and *to rise from the dead. . .repentance and remission of sins should be preached in his name. . .* (Luke 24:46-47). His death and resurrection were necessary for our salvation. The King James Version uses the word "behoved" which means "must." He links three things together—His death, His resurrection, and telling the message. Without the latter, His death and resurrection would be of no avail.

Witnessing is a must. People around us at home and overseas are lost, lost, lost. Without the Savior they are doomed to a Christless eternity. Does a passion for their souls grip you? Do you feel the yearnings of God Who so loved that He gave His son?

Have you sensed the anguished cry of Jesus, *O Jerusalem, Jerusalem. . .how often would I have gathered thy children together, as a hen doth gather her brood under her wings, and ye would not!* (Luke 13:34)?

Hear the burden of Paul. *I could wish that myself were accursed from Christ for my brethren* (Romans 9:3).

Listen to the soul-stirring plea of Moses: *Oh, this people have sinned. . .Yet now, if thou wilt forgive their sin; and if not blot me, I pray thee, out of thy book which thou hast written* (Exodus 32:31-32).

Don't let your loved one, your neighbor, the person you work with or the one you trade with be able to say as the Psalmist stated, *No man cared for my soul and sin. . .*(Psalm 142:4).

A confrontation with God will burn a passion for the lost into your heart. Do not let the flame die out! Communicate your faith!

Seeing God not only gives us a sense of His holiness and a passion for lost souls but challenges us to a discipleship clothed with humility.

All Christians are called to the ministry. Ministry is to be carried on by people, not programs; by someone, not something. Discipleship produces ministry.

Discipleship makes all of life sacred. Devotion to Christ is more than a heart experience; it affects behavior. The Christian believes and behaves.

A believer becomes a disciple when he submits to the authority of God's Word, acknowledging the right of Christ to rule over him, and puts himself completely at Christ's disposal. Someone has said it does not take much of a person to be a disciple, but it takes all of him there is.

Our Lord's teaching presents the concept that love and service are interchangeable. There is no virtue in compulsory obedience. Our service in true discipleship is prompted by consuming love.

Love for Christ and His church demands commitment by devotion, disciplined living, discipleship, servanthood, steadfastness in doctrine, and loyalty to God's Word.

Our Lord taught servanthood. He declared, *Whosoever will be great among you. . .let him be your servant: even as the Son of man came not to be ministered unto, but to minister* (Matthew 20:26-28).

He also declared, *And whosoever shall compel thee to go a mile, go with him twain* (Matthew 5:41). Take care that you do not become so upset about going the first mile that you lose the reward of a second mile experience. The second mile requires discipline, but is not legalistic and there is joy in doing the unrequired.

From the Day of Pentecost there has never been a spiritual awakening which was not birthed through prayer, and no spiritual awakening has continued when prayer has declined. Prayer brings a hunger for the Word, both the Living Word and the written Word. The theme statement for the children of God is, "I will pray. I believe." In heaven-sent revival the Bible is always preeminent. "The higher the temperature of revival, the stronger must be the scriptual caldron in which the medicine is prepared." Revival fires must be governed by Scripture. The Bible is the final authority for faith and practice. The New Testament presents a strong plea for sound doctrine.

Doctrine is necessary to communicate the Christian faith (Acts 20:20-27; Ephesians 4:14). Doctrine is necessary to defend the Christian faith (Philippians 1:17 & 27; Jude 3; Colossians 4:6; I Peter 3:15).

Will you join me in praying, "Lord, revive thy work"? As we do, we can face this year with confidence because we will have a new awareness of God's holiness, a motivation to reach the lost, and a desire to be the kind of followers our Lord needs as witnesses in today's world. If we are to remain strong and effective in our world, we must maintain prayer meetings, prayer closets, and the prayer life of the church. For prayer is indispensable to the ongoing blessing of God. Nothing will compensate for the spiritual power that we gain through fasting and prayer. If we do not fast and pray, we will be powerless as individuals.

Prayer is a conversation. The first Old Testament record of conversation between man and God is found in Genesis 3:8. Adam and Eve heard the voice of God as He was "walking in the garden." There is no way to know what was in God's heart when He created man in His own image and chose to communicate with him. But He did. That communication continued in the New Testament. Jesus said,

When ye pray. . .pray ye: Our Father. . . (Matthew 6:7-9). That expresses God's desire to maintain a close relationship with man.

Prayer and fasting is both a duty and a privilege. In fact, Scripture encourages us to make our lives expressions of prayer and praise: *That we should be to the praise of his glory. . .*(Ephesians 1:12), and *that ye should shew forth the praises of him who hath called you out of darkness. . .* (I Peter 2:9). The Psalmist said, *I have set the LORD always before me. . .* (Psalm 16:8).

Old Testament prayers give us a pattern for praying. Old Testament people prayed, confessing sin, asking for forgiveness and renewal, and vowing faithfulness to God.

In the New Testament Jesus became our example in vigilance and faithfulness. He exhorted His disciples to watch and pray. In ministry and teaching He showed us that effectiveness in prayer and relationship to God depend upon relationships with others. Forgiveness comes by prayer (I John 1:9), and prayer is effective only when we are forgiving (Mark 11:26). The continuous flow of divine mercy and grace to us makes us forgiving. Forgiven, we forgive.

The purpose of prayer is to restore and maintain right relationships with God and man. Once we are right with God and man, prayer becomes a vehicle for petition, thanksgiving, and praise. Prayer becomes "effectual" states James 5:16 when we are energized by the Holy Spirit.

So prayer is a relationship!

THE POWER OF PRAYER

What is supposed to happen when we pray? What do the Scriptures teach? Prayer changes many things, but the first change is in the person praying. The power of prayer does not depend upon our physical posture. It does not depend upon your area. Jesus told the Samaritan woman that God was not in this place or another, but He is met *in spirit and truth* (John 4:23).

The power of prayer does not depend upon the number of people praying. At times we must pray alone. At other times two or three should agree in prayer. I have heard thousands of people pray together. But the effectiveness of prayer does not depend upon having a certain number of people present. The power of prayer is determined in part by the earnestness and sincerity of the person praying, once scriptural conditions have been met.

The power and effectiveness of prayer do depend upon our willingness to spend time in the presence of our Heavenly Father. Waiting and patience are postures to receive. We do not pray simply to tell God something; there is nothing we can tell Him. Prayer requires time and commitment to a relationship. Jesus said, *If you believe, you will receive whatever you ask for in prayer* (Matthew 21:22, NIV). Does this mean we will get from God everything we want? Does this mean we can demand that God's will conform to ours? Let us also take the words of I John 5:14, *This is the assurance we have in approaching God: that if we ask anything according to his will, he hears us* (NIV).

God wants to give to us things that conform to His will and contribute to our spiritual maturity. We can expect God to hear our prayers as we maintain a right relationship with Him, and say with Jesus Christ, *My food is to do the will of him who sent me and to finish his work* (John 4:34, NIV). Our prayers do not change the mind of God. We cannot, by praying, move Him to be more merciful than He already is. But prayer will condition us to receive His boundless mercy and grace. When we are aligned with God's will, we have absolute assurance as to the dependability of prayer. We know He hears us when we pray. We have confidence in His good will toward us. We then pray, "Our Father," knowing we are in the presence of the One who knows us best and knows what is best for us.

THE DESIRABLILITY OF PRAYER

The Holy Spirit continually urges us toward higher plateaus of discipleship. Too often our prayerlessness precludes a positive response. The earnest believer will be found in prayer meeting and prayer groups. God will be found by those who diligently seek Him. I am concerned for children and youth. I covet deep spiritual experiences in prayer for them. I pray God will raise up each generation with a deep spiritual prayer experience.

After New Testament Christians prayed, the place was shaken (Acts 4:31). Prayer is not vain babbling or simply flinging verbal requests heavenward. Prayer is yielding our wills to the will of our Heavenly Father so the channels of divine power are opened to do God's will. Between prayers that run from adoring whispers to torrential outpourings of verbal fire can be prayers that are calm and comforting, intelligent and eloquent, routine and heartwarming. Prayer can be praise or thanksgiving;

supplication or intercession. It can be soundless, as was Hannah's; and it can be wordless, as was the sinner woman's who washed Jesus' feet with her tears.

But there is one kind of prayer that is distinctive in its unrelenting concentration on one specific object and request. Such was the prayer of Elijah in his seven-time supplication for rain; and such was the prayer of Jesus in Gethsemane, of which the record states, *He. . .prayed the third time, saying the same words* (Matthew 26:44). It seems certain that Hebrews 5:7 refers to Jesus' experience in the Garden. *Who in the days of his flesh. . .offered up prayers and supplication with strong crying and tears. . .*

While no Scripture passage supports any idea that all of Jesus' praying was of this nature, yet it clearly shows there were occasions when His praying was marked by extreme intensity and profound emotional involvement.

It seems to me this kind of praying has become increasingly and regrettably scarce in recent years. Granted that loud praying, per se, has no Bible premium placed upon it and can actually be as distasteful and futile as the Pharisees' long praying. Granted that the decibel output of the supplicant's voice cannot necessarily be equated with spiritual power. The stubborn fact remains that a human being in extreme distress—whether threatened with drowning, trapped in a burning building, or lost in a forest—never carefully modulates his voice when crying for help.

That there exists a clear relationship between the degree of feeling within and the sound of the voice is not hard to establish. When Jesus stood before the tomb of Lazarus, He *cried with a loud voice, Lazarus, come forth* (John 11:43). Certainly it was not for the sake of Lazarus that Jesus' voice was loud, for the loudest voice cannot alone awaken the dead. I believe it was due to the tremendous surge of divine power that swept up and out of His innermost being and was transmitted to the dead man by and through His words, *Lazarus, come forth.*

In our understandably negative reaction to incidents and individuals that seem to violate the Bible rule, *Let all things be done decently and in order* (I Corinthians 14:40), we should beware lest we overreact and muzzle genuine travail, stifle spontaneity, quench Holy Ghost praying, and place people in spiritual straitjackets. This is not intended as a defense of unseemly screaming, yelling, or bellowing. It is simply a plea for the true liberty of the Spirit in our prayer meetings and altar services. The very real danger is that we destroy the wheat with the tares.

We Pentecostals, who claim the identical experience enjoyed by Christians in the Book of Acts, have a unique responsibility to validate our claim by duplicating their record. Most of our concepts of the church in its daily life and activities are drawn from the Book of Acts. This should most certainly include their practice and methods of prayer.

While several detailed descriptions of apostolic prayer meetings can be found in Acts, perhaps the most impressive is the report of the occasion of which it is recorded, *When they had prayed, the place was shaken where they were assembled* (Acts 4:31). Some translations use even stronger language: *The place where they were was violently moved — the building in which they had gathered rocked to and fro;* and *the building where they were meeting shook.* Is it possible to imagine a prayer meeting that produced such a result could have been marked by a hushed and funeral atmosphere, by general inhibition and restraint, and by painful pauses and solemn silences?

Hardly, when the record plainly tells us that *they lifted up their voice to God with one accord* (Acts 4:24).

Two facts clearly emerge: (1) they prayed in unison; (2) they prayed aloud. Such a prayer meeting might have greatly pleased the celebrated Baptist preacher, Charles Spurgeon. Spurgeon chided the Methodists of his day for their loss of glory and freedom in prayer. The following ringing plea is from the pen of the eloquent preacher:

> "How I delight to listen to a brother who talks to God simply and from his heart; and I must confess I have no small liking to those rare old-fashioned Methodist prayers, who are now quite out-of-date.
>
> Mother, who was converted in a Methodist church, often said, "Our Methodist churches, for the most part, are getting too fine and respectable nowadays; too genteel to allow prayers such as once made the walls to ring and ring again. Oh, for a revival of those glorious violent prayers which flew like hot shot against the battlements of heaven" (Matthew 11:12).
>
> Oh, for more moving of the posts of the doors in vehemence; more thundering at the gates

of mercy! I would sooner attend a prayer meeting where there were groans and cries all over the place, and shouts of "hallelujah!" than be in your polite church assemblies where everything is dull as death and decorous as the white-washed sepulcher! Oh, for more of the power of God; the body, soul, and spirit working together, the whole man being aroused and startled up to the highest pitch of intensity—to wrestle with the Most High. Such, I have no doubt, was the prayer of Jesus when on the cold mountainside.

If the old revivalists, long decades before the latter rain outpouring, could express their feelings about prayer with such potent words as vehemence, thundering, groans, cries, shouts, arousal, and intensity, how can we possibly fear them?

What glorious revivals, what profound renewals, what transformations in individuals and churches would ensue if the situation described in Judges 21:2 were to be reenacted in every church across the nation; *And the people came to the house of God, and abode there till even before God, and lifted up their voices, and wept sore.*

This would bring a profound moving of the Holy Spirit in a Holy Spirit revival.

9

GROANS, AGONY & TRAVAIL

For we know that the whole creation groaneth and travaileth in pain together until now.
Romans 8:22

"Our creation is subject to frustration. . ." Living on a planet under the curse poses problems and frustrations for all created things. But it is not final. When Christ returns to redeem the earth, the curse will be removed. Then even the fields shall be joyful and the wilderness glad. Trees shall clap their hands in that glad day.

Nonetheless, it must be admitted that even we believers experience heavyheartedness. But why? Certainly not from the weight of guilt or fear of judgment. At least we should not, for *there is therefore now no condemnation to them which are in Christ Jesus* (Romans 8:11). Nor should we suffer from the sense of hopelessness that grips the world. We've read the last chapter of the Book and can see beyond the present chaos. Yet it is true that our hearts ache at times. I suppose it's partly because we witness sin and the heavy toll of misery it exacts on lives all around us.

While living in Florida, we witnessed many problems. On one occasion we were leaving the office, when the telephone rang.

"T.V. 45"

"Sister Murphy."

"Yes."

"This is Harry."

"Yes."

"I need to talk to you and your husband."

"When."

"NOW."

By the tone of his voice I knew he had a problem. "We will wait."

When he arrived, he took an envelope out of his pocket. We could see they were legal papers. He lay them on my desk. He said, "My wife is sueing me for a divorce, because I love Jesus!!!"

All the blood seemed to have drained from his face. His lips trembled as he said, "I need prayer. I have brought some of this upon myself. She is not all the problem. I did many things that were wrong."

As I looked at this man who was devastated from the loss of his wife and children, he said, "I will give my wife and children all the material things they ask, but, I do not want to give up Jesus." Both my husband and I knew if God did not move in Harry's life he would not make it, and would go down under the load. Before he left we prayed that God would give him strength and determination to stay true to God.

We made our time available to him at any hour he needed prayer or counseling.

We willingly invested many hours in intercessory prayer. It made us sad as we saw him alone and brokenhearted. I am sure it was the hardest battle Harry ever fought. Many times the Spirit of God would burden our heart to pray for him. There were times the Lord would awaken us in the wee hours of the night, showing us that Satan was coming against him. We would take authority over the devil and pray for the comfort of the Holy Ghost to overshadow him and keep him from all temptations.

Travail in intercession for a person gives you a feeling that you have an investment in their life and you must protect them from the attacts of Satan.

We visited him a short time ago. His face radiated with the joy of the Lord. Through the years God has given him strength to resist the temptations that Satan has thrown in his path. He is now established in a full gospel church serving as an elder and Sunday School teacher.

It took intercessory prayer, and long hours of prayer.

Paul explained it in his letter to the Corinthians: *For we that are in this tabernacle do groan, being burdened* (II Corinthians 5:4). These "tabernacles" or bodies of ours surely have their limitations and struggles. It's understandable why *we ourselves groan within ourselves, waiting for the adoption. . .the redemption of our body* (Romans 8:23). That is why, though we are redeemed, Christ's coming for the Church is spoken of as the day of our redemption.

Jesus said, *Lift up your heads; for your redemption draweth nigh* (Luke 21:28). For our bodies shall undergo a miraculous transformation. Suddenly, in less time than it takes to blink your eye, all painful arthritis, persistent backaches, and splitting headaches will be gone! There will be no high blood pressure, heart pain, or dreaded cancer in our glorified bodies. All frustrating physical problems will be forever removed.

When prayer is offered in an agony of intense desire, God moves in mighty power to meet His people's needs.

The ancient olympic games, held first in the shadow of Mount Olympus, added a number of words to the English language. For example, the place of the contests was called "agony." The training was rigid. My husband was an athletic director while in the army. In directing the soldiers he told them, "There's agony in winning." There is physical pain in training and in competition. Without some agony a person cannot win. Since the competition is stiff, each man is up against the best qualified man in the army. So they exert themselves beyond their own physical abilities. They try so hard it hurts. Prayer never comes easily. So the principle applies equally well in the spiritual life. There's more to prayer than feeling good.

GROANS

The word "groan" means "to make, i.e. to sigh, murmur, pray inaudibly."

Likewise the Spirit also helpeth our infirmities: for we know not what we should pray

for as we ought: but the Spirit itself maketh intercession for us with groanings which cannot be uttered (Romans 8:26).
1. The word "likewise" refers to what is said before. Read verse 23. It is in the same manner that the Holy Spirit helps us by groaning.
2. One of the meanings of the word, "infirmity" is feebleness of body. We may not know what the trouble is, but the Holy Spirit intercedes with groanings. God hears the groanings and healing is ours.
3. There will always be the need for the Holy Spirit to intercede with groanings. We may know the will of God, but only the Holy Spirit knows how to effectively present the need. There are circumstances in which we are not sure of how to pray. We need the groaning of the Holy Spirit in intercession.

Divine compassion says, "I feel how you feel." And it brings deliverance. Jesus felt compassion for Mary and Martha as He groaned within and also wept (John 11:33-35). It is weeping with them that weep (Romans 12:15). His compassion brought deliverance.

In adverse circumstances or conditions the Holy Spirit intercedes with groanings. It is to make us like Jesus. The idea is to get us to respond as Jesus Himself would respond. It is to change us inwardly so the natural flow outwardly will be in accordance with God's will.

In my experience, I often have inner burdens and groanings when I know someone is in trouble or has a need. I appreciate the opportunity to be used of God in this manner.

We must identify with the one for whom we are interceding. Jesus identified with Mary and Martha in the death of Lazarus. The Jews and the sisters were groaning and weeping. He groaned within and wept. They went to the grave and Jesus raised Lazarus from the dead.

Romans 12:15 brings into focus the idea of identification with others. *Rejoice with them that do rejoice, and weep with them that weep.* The real believer can go from the house of rejoicing and go to the house of weeping and weep with them. We may not know how or what to ask in prayer so that our prayer will correspond with our real needs. It is then that the Holy Spirit moves us with groanings which cannot be expressed in words and helps us direct our desires to the proper objects. Also the Holy Spirit helps us to be specific as a part of the groanings. These groanings and yearnings are according to the will of God and expresses His care for us. Although we cannot understand the groanings (Greek, sigh), they are intelligible to God. He always responds.

Paul identified with the Jews that he might gain the Jews. Paul identified to them as without law (being without law to God, but under law to Christ) that he might gain them that are without law. To the weak he became as weak that he might gain the weak. He said that he was made all things to all men, that he by all means might save some (I Corinthians 9:10-22). It is identification with the person in need.

AGONY

There is agony along with the ecstasy. The word agony is used twice in prayer in the New Testament. It is translated "laboring fervently" in Colossians 4:12, but is left virtually untranslated in Luke 22:44, *and being in an agony he (Jesus) prayed more earnestly.* Have you ever thought of prayer as a warfare? To Jesus in Gethesmane it represented all the anxiety, struggle, and mental pain that we associate with the term "agony. " To accept the will of God which meant shame and suffering was not easy. The cross was repulsive. The pure soul of Jesus was praying to the Father, *if it be thy will let this cup pass from me.* The struggle in the Garden was no sham fight; it represented mortal combat between the Prince of life and the prince of darkness.

Epaphras, following the steps of the master, gave himself to intercession for the saints (Colossians 4:12). He toiled in prayer and thus displayed his love, and burning concern for his brethren in Christ. He prayed that the will of God might be done in the maturing lives of His people. The greatest thing in the world is to live as God wills us to live.

Prayer has many facets. There may be loving submission and confession. It may be worship and praise. It is not always asking for divine favors. Sometimes it is just an affirmation of comfort and assurance. All the various kinds of prayer are blessed and necessary. For we are in a spiritual battle. There are human needs that call for divine intervention and there is an enemy who strongly opposes all that is good. Prayer is a warfare that calls for some agony in order to overcome Satan's evil forces.

That is why the Scriptures tell us to *put on the whole armour of God, that ye may be able to stand against the wiles of the devil* (Ephesians 6:11). We are in a warfare with wicked spirits.

The Word continues: *For we wrestle not*

against flesh and blood, but against principalities, against powers, against the rulers of the darkness of this world, against spiritual wickedness in high places (Ephesians 6:12).

The struggle is not won without pain. Prayer has always been the price of spiritual victory. We read in Galatians 4:19, *My little children, of whom I travail in birth again until Christ be formed in you.* Travail is a spiritual activity. It is an intense suffering in the inner man. It is comparable to the birth pangs of natural childbirth. When I was a child, the Christians involved in the prayer of travail would suffer until you would think their heart would literally break.

In my family, I have heard this cry of travail for revival, and the salvation of lost loved ones and friends.

There are times when we approach the throne, but we do not know how to pray as we ought. It is then that the Holy Spirit takes over with groanings and travail that cannot be uttered. The travailings are understood by God and our needs are met.

TRAVAIL

There are times during groans, agony, travail and intercession the Holy Spirit will lead us to the one in need.

One morning during family devotion, Mother entered into the Spirit of intercession and travail. She did not know for whom she was interceding. After a time of agonizing in the Spirit, she was bidden to arise and "Go." She answered, "Lord, where must I go?" Again He spoke the word, "Go." This happened several times; and each time she would answer, "Where, Lord?" At last the voice said, "Abraham went out not knowing where he was going." She answered, "Lord, I too, will trust your leading hand."

She arose from her knees, brushed her hair and got into the car. She drove slowly meditating on the goodness of God whom she was trying to obey. Passing through the business district she drove into a section of town that she knew nothing about. She still did not know where she was to go, but trusted God to guide her. It seemed as if an unseen hand was driving the car. Finally she came to a short dead end street. Automatically the car seemed to turn to the right. She said the presence of God was very real!

On this street was a simple little cottage. Going to the door, she knocked and a man invited her in. Introducing herself, she told him she was on an errand for the Lord. She was told the mother was bedfast, and the father had received an injury on the job. Lying motionless on a bed in the same room was their twelve year old daughter, who looked like a corpse. She had sleeping disease. It was a heartrending scene. The parents did not attend church. Mother testified her experience of healing. The lady listened with interest. Then Mother related how the Lord dealt with her while having devotions. "The Holy Spirit did not make known to me where he was sending me. He just said, 'Go!' I obeyed and he directed me to your home. Would you like for me to pray?"

"You may if you want to," replied the mother. Kneeling by her bedside, she told the lady that Jesus wanted to save her from sin and heal her body. When she prayed, heaven came down and the house was filled with the glory of God. The Lord gave the lady complete deliverance from sin and healing for her body.

Glancing at the father, she saw that the Holy Spirit had touched his heart. She prayed with him and the Lord saved and healed him.

Mother's attention turned to the pale face of the little girl. She walked over and prayed, "O God, awaken this child!" Instantly, her eyes opened and God healed her.

That family became some of the best people in our church and remained loyal to the Lord!

Romans 8:26-27 says, *Likewise the Spirit also helpeth our infirmities: for we know not what we should pray for as we ought: but the Spirit itself maketh intercession for us with groanings which cannot be uttered. And he that searcheth the hearts knoweth what is the mind of the Spirit, because he maketh intercession for the saints according to the will of God.*

Many Christians are sick, poor and defeated. They need a revelation of the Word of God in their lives. This is where intercession comes in. The word "helpeth," in Romans 8:26, literally means that the Holy Spirit takes hold together with us against the forces of darkness which have come against another person.

The Gospel is the power of God unto salvation. The preaching of the Gospel brings the power of God on the scene. This is why the Apostle Paul wrote Timothy saying, *I EXHORT therefore, that, first of all, supplications, prayers, intercessions, and giving of thanks, be made for all men* (I Timothy 2:1). Travail prepares the hearts of the people to receive the Gospel because it tears down the strongholds of deception that Satan has brought against them. Revivals have never been the result of good preaching. The preaching of the Gospel with power is the result of prayer. It takes the anointing of the Holy Spirit to cause changes in the hearts of the people. Travail is the tool that activates that anointing. No matter who you are in the Body of Christ, minister or lay person, you can have an eternal effect on the lives of others through your travail. All it takes is a decision to start praying specifically for a given body of people—a family, town, city, county, state, or a nation. Do not wait for a burden or a feeling to motivate you to pray. Jesus was not moved by His feelings. He was moved with compassion. He did what He did because God told Him to do it. God's word says, *Go ye into all the world and preach the gospel to every creature* (Mark 16:15). As an act of your will, allow yourself to be used by the Holy Spirit to pray the perfect will of God for someone else. Through your travail, you have contacted the Father in their behalf. Now go contact them in Jesus' behalf. Go and preach the Gospel of Jesus Christ to them! The Holy Spirit will work through your spirit to bring about a change in them. Your travailing prayer had been doing spiritual warfare against the evil forces that have blinded their minds and have influenced their decisions and actions.

Travailing prayer is one of the highest expressions of love. It is impossible to be selfish when travailing because travailing prayer is always for another person's benefit. It is putting a halt to the influence of Satan in their life so that they can walk in the fullness of the redemption that God has provided. First Timothy 2:4 says that *it is God who will have all men to be saved and come unto the knowledge of the truth.* The truth is that, through the cross, Jesus destroyed the power of Satan, sin, sickness, poverty, fear and all the curse of the law. It is the will of God that all men live this life free from the influence of the law of sin and death (Romans 8:2).

Testimony Letters

Dear Sister Murphy,

I have just finished reading your book, "Miracles and the Sumrall Family." I have laughed, cried and praised God all through the book. God is so good to us.

All through your book you give God all the glory. Not once do you take credit for the miracles that were performed...

Each time I read a book so inspired of God, I thank Him for people who will follow His will.

My life has been touched by your book. You are a true soldier for God...

S.F.

Dear Sister Leona,

Over and over again as I watched Jimmy Swaggart I would hear him mention Leona Sumrall coming to Ferriday, LA to start a church etc., etc.

Praise God I purchased your book "Miracles and the Sumrall Family" in the vestibule of one of our local churches. Oh Sister Leona, how I love your book. It was written so good and such an easy style. I love reading and hearing about miracles. Praise God I pray that I too could have such a strong faith as you have, to be a faithful prayer warrior. I want to share your book with my Spirit-filled Christian friends. I know that they will be blessed by it just as I have been.

C.B.
Swannanoa, N.C.

YOU, TOO, CAN BE SAVED!

I ask you: If you're not born again, if you are not *sure* where you'd go if you were to die RIGHT NOW, please ask Jesus into your heart. He will give you peace, and joy, and hope!

You need a personal Savior, a personal commitment to Him who is able and willing to forgive you of ALL your sins. Pray this Sinner's Prayer, and really MEAN it.

"Lord Jesus, I am a sinner. I believe that you died and rose from the tomb to save me from my sins. Forgive me by Your grace for all the sins that I have committed. Wash me with Your blood, and I shall be clean. I ask You into my heart right now. Be my Savior and my guide forever. Amen."

In your flesh, you may not FEEL any different. But, the Word of God tells us that you are now a New Creature, and old things are passed away and forgiven. You are no longer under condemnation. You are in Christ Jesus and you now walk after the Spirit (Romans 8:1, II Corinthians 5:17, I John 2:12, Luke 7:47).

Now that you have become a child of God, please write and tell us and we'll send you some literature to help you walk daily with the Lord. Write to:

LeSEA, Inc.
P.O. Box 12
South Bend, Indiana 46624.
24-hour Prayerline: (219) 291-1010

Other Books by Leona Sumrall Murphy:

- A Teenager Who Dared To Obey God
- Miracles And The Sumrall Family
- Healed Of Muscular Dystrophy
- The Marriage Triangle